Praise for
Chaplain's Walk: The Spiritual Side of Medicine

"This book will bring you both smiles and tears, an amazing read with stories we can all learn from. Having worked in healthcare for the past forty years both in clinical and leadership roles, I found Jan Moberg's *Chaplain's Walk* a touching and insightful summary of the impact we as "providers" have in the lives of individuals. This sharing of experiences and very personal moments is not one directed only to healthcare providers rather one that will resonate with all individuals as it focuses on the impact of relationships. . . . Having had the pleasure of working with Jan in the acute care setting, I know the value her wisdom, presence, and strong belief system has brought to our patients, their families, and our caregivers. Jan displays a calming wisdom in all she does which I feel is well captured through the experiences shared. . . . As we progress down life's journeys, we may often lose sight of not only the acts of kindness we provided to others but also the gifts we have received in return from so many.

"*Chaplain's Walk* offers life's most precious lessons. . . . Small kindness matters. Never underestimate the strength of silence and listening. Learn from the past to better the future. And most of all, cherish every moment with your loved ones. *Chaplain's Walk is a great read for all!*"

—Darlene Stephenson, Hospital President and COO

"Throughout the past two decades, an entire subculture has existed around the consumption of hospital-based shows in television format. Life, death, drama, and disasters have moved individuals from laughter to tears. Without fail, a glaring truth is painfully missing in many of these series—the profundity sickness and death have upon the human soul. We all walk through this life as if we are invincible, focused wholly on the here and now. However, the thought of eternity and the state of the soul never becomes clearer than alongside the bed of a patient as last breaths are drawn. In the moment of absolute loss, one cannot escape the ramifications of a life that was here moments before and the questions of what has become of that soul in the hereafter. As a surgical provider, I can attest there is a tendency to harden one's inner being to withstand such losses in the medical field—prevent the pain, avoid the loss, ignore the ramifications of the temporary nature of our being. How does a patient or family navigate these issues when life is crashing down around them?

"Enter, Jan Moberg and the *Chaplain's Walk*. The chaplain is a character you'll likely never see on the big screen TV hospital drama. When you consider the eternality of the soul of man, one could argue its state and condition are of greater significance than the life and limb medical professionals may be trying to save. The chaplain is the one who walks the difficult road, wages in the waters of despair, and navigates the rapids of ruination. What Jan Moberg has given readers in the *Chaplain's Walk* is truly a gift. Jan takes readers alongside that deathbed and lays her emotions and thoughts bare for all to experience. Sharing the stories of others in such tumultuous situations caries great significance, but Jan does not stop there. Jan opens up regarding her own personal health struggles as well as her demanding role as the end-of-life care provider for her dear mother. So today, I dare you, open these pages and take a few steps in the walk of a chaplain, and I assure you your perspective of life, death, and medical care will never be the same."

—**Dr. J Marshall Green** III DDS FACS

"Despite the moon changing phases throughout time, we only get to see one side. As a physician working in a fast-paced, ever-changing hospital, I focus on my patients' physical and mental illness the most, and seldom have the time to see the other side—the spiritual side of medicine. Jan introduces the readers to a variety of heartfelt, warm, but sometimes extremely emotional stories. This leaves me with not a physical power of healing, but an experience on the spiritual and mental side of healing. This book is a must read for anyone with loved ones who have a critical illness or are nearing end-of-life. No matter if you are religious or not, love, caring, and understanding are powerful tools used during the difficult times of our lives, which *Chaplain's Walk* emphasizes, the other side of the moon."

—**Dr. Xia Li**, Internal Medicine

"*Chaplain's Walk* is amazing. Jan's love for God is palpable and made me ponder my own spirituality. I too have deep religious beliefs but lack the grace to portray my faith as eloquently as she has. I laughed and cried reading the personal experiences she shared so beautifully. Once again, I am reminded of the reason I chose to become a nurse so late in life! *Chaplain's Walk: The Spiritual Side of Medicine* inspired me to be a better person!"

—**Patricia M. Orgain, BSN, RN, CEN, CN IV**, Clinical Care Lead at Emergency Department, PNAP Co-Chair

"Our culture creates a split between body and spirit, but hospital chaplain Jan Moberg holds the two together. In *Chaplain's Walk,* she tells powerful and personal stories from a quarter-century of ministry, illustrating how the best medical care requires spiritual care. Healing happens when body and spirit are treated together, with insight and compassion, even at the end of life."

—**Henry G. Brinton**, pastor and author of the mystery novel *City of Peace*

"*Chaplain's Walk* brings to light the very essence of walking in a chaplain's shoes, both emotionally and spiritually, discovering that this light shines in all of us throughout our lives. Jan Moberg brings insight to the reader of how empathy, care, and compassion changes our lives."

—**Lesley C. Blankenship**, Care Management Specialist

"In my life as a pastor, I often felt inadequate when faced with pastoral situations involving spiritual counsel and medical struggles. Pediatrics, oncology, and palliative care bring unique challenges to visiting church clergy. Jan Moberg's book, *Chaplain's Walk: The Spiritual Side of Medicine*, contains profound wisdom and humility on how to navigate these turbulent waters. Jan is a storyteller, not a lecturer. She sharpens your mind while softening your heart. Every caregiver needing guidance or comfort, whether a spiritual or medical professional, or simply an adult caring for an aging parent or a special needs child, needs to read *Chaplain's Walk: The Spiritual Side of Medicine*."

—**Rev. Dr. Hoyt A. Byrum**, PCUS, coauthor of *The Chase*

"I was very excited to read *Chaplain's Walk: The Spiritual Side of Medicine.* I was not prepared for the emotions the book evoked; I laughed, I cried, I re-read many sections, because they were that important. Jan Moberg does an excellent job of telling her story and the path that she has traveled. I worked in the field of patent and employee engagement for eighteen years and could relate to so many of these experiences. I will read *Chaplain's Walk* again and again."

—**Peggy Frizzell**, Hospital Service Excellence, Ret.

"*Chaplain's Walk: The Spiritual Side of Medicine* is a phenomenal work capturing experiences spanning the better part of a lifetime commitment of service and work, assisting individuals at a critical time. Expressing eloquently raw emotional times when one is facing end-of-life events, and equally expressing when one escapes that event through medical science, unpredictably emotional, *Chaplain's Walk is* not only for the patient but all friends and family members. Illness and dying is a time we understand perhaps the least, and everyone handles those challenges differently. It is a time when medical folks are sometimes out of solutions. *Chaplain's Walk* illustrates patient assistance and the idea that family is sometimes no more complicated than being present, even without words. It is a gift to fulfill a need in the least understood period in a person's existence. *Chaplain's Walk* helps one understand how to bridge that gap. It captures emotion to the core, and at the same time is enlightening. Involved in a chaplain capacity, I can appreciate the author's experiences and only hope to someday achieve that level of understanding. I would encourage this read for everyone in the medical field and beyond. It makes one wonder, think, and understand."

—**Frank Chebalo,** CBI, ABI, CMSBB, CBC, CM&AP,
Business Owner, Volunteer Chaplain

"I have been a nurse for almost forty years, the majority of my time spent in a hospital. *Chaplain's Walk* is a true gift to those of us called to serve in healthcare. It reminded me why I love being a nurse and how incredibly blessed I am to be part of patients' lives at their most vulnerable times."

—**Jan Phillips**, DNP, RN, CENP, CPPS, VP of Nursing,
Chief Nursing Executive

"I am a long time Episcopalian and have been part of men's religious study groups for over ten years, reading everything from books by Richard Rohr to Rabbi Telushkin. *Chaplain's Walk* is absolutely something I will recommend for our group and friends who are looking for a fresh look at spirituality. *Chaplain's Walk* takes you on a trip to the darkest corners of life and shines God's bright light. Jan's thoughtful exploration of her profession helped me immensely with life's toughest question—how to cope with death. I greatly appreciated her candid descriptions of real human interaction in the most difficult emotional settings. Her willingness to share her personal scars and faith challenges gives the book even more credibility. On another level, the book makes a compelling argument that spirituality needs to be embraced as an integral part of our healthcare delivery system. I think this is summed up best by my favorite line from the book; "what one cannot make sense of, faith will make possible to cope with." *Chaplain's Walk* is a journey well worth taking!"

—Jim Noel

"Jan Moberg's must-read, *Chaplain's Walk: The Spiritual Side of Medicine,* is by turns both heart-warming and heart-rending. Moberg harnesses the key elements of wit and wisdom as she takes us on a journey into end-of-life matters, from both her personal and professional perspectives. Read this book and learn from one of the best!"

—Delores Vinson, Retired Educator

"While reading *Chaplain's Walk*, I realized how this book could be an important tool for any hospital or medical staff office employee, from administrators, doctors, and nurses to any other persons who might come into contact with patients and their families. Jan reminds us in her writings that the contact made with any patient comes with the responsibility to treat them as people, not cases, and to offer compassion and hope, healing and assisting them. By helping a patient or their family spiritually, that person has more value than simply their illness, and Jan makes that clear with the personal experiences she shares. . . . Jan makes it obvious, drawing on her beliefs and understanding of what God has called us all to do for others, we can be a beacon in even the most devastating situation. . . . Today's world is filled with intelligent, talented, ambitious individuals. The individual who is all that but also understands what Jan is expressing in *Chaplain's Walk* will be a treasure in any healthcare situation. This should be required reading for all medical students."

—Gwendolyn Appleton, Hospital Volunteer Coordinator

Chaplain's Walk: The Spiritual Side of Medicine

by Jan Moberg

© Copyright 2021 Jan Moberg

ISBN 978-1-64663-549-8

Published by

köehlerbooks™

3705 Shore Drive
Virginia Beach, VA 23455
800-435-4811
www.koehlerbooks.com

CHAPLAIN'S WALK
THE SPIRITUAL SIDE OF MEDICINE

JAN MOBERG

VIRGINIA BEACH
CAPE CHARLES

Dedication

The heart of *Chaplain's Walk* was created by the patients, families, and hospital staff I have met during my twenty-five-year career in chaplaincy, ethics, and patient advocacy. The support of my husband, adult children, friends, and co-workers and their belief in my ability to justly recount these sacred moments has been invaluable, especially as life's challenges became intensely personal. While I am unable to thank those who have journeyed from this world, one day as we gather in peace and triumph, I will be given the opportunity to express my gratitude for the privilege of having been able to accompany them, however briefly, on this side of Heaven.

May God bless each reader who engages in the telling of a *Chaplain's Walk*, and considers the mysteries and faith of *the Spiritual Side of Medicine* . . .

Many times, we look back and see we could have trusted God. Though we never look back and question why we did.

Table of Contents

Foreword

As in many workplace relationships, I really met Jan at least two years after we were officially acquainted. We had been introduced, and I knew her role. I listened regularly to her reports of patient perspectives, and I knew her to be professional, caring, and positive.

But as in all the best friendships, there came that moment. Standing at a nurse's station, surely a place we had both been many times before, a chance comment somehow opened up a personal window. It was probably one of her many expressions of empathy about a patient or staff member. Usually these would pass by in the chatter of the day, but for some reason, the comment resonated, and we began to share—*really* share, that instant when you let another person into your story and give each other your trust with things that are meaningful.

I don't recall the beginning, but at the end of the conversation, we had a new depth to our fellowship, and I had been renewed, the start of the day seemingly chaotic and busy, now refreshed. I walked away knowing I had been gifted, that her spirit had given me some of its strength, and my perspective had been lifted.

I realized with a new vision that Jan was a giver, and that her titles in no way conveyed her true work among our hospital staff. Jan carries a countenance that is smiling, open, and friendly. She is inviting all comers to the well of her caring. She spends days replenishing patients, visitors, and staff, and she never seems to run dry. But the true appreciation for that apparently effortless talent comes when you are able to know the path of self-realization and struggle that has powered the light she shines. She lets you know she is real, revealing her own frailties. And therein lies her greatest gift, sharing her story so that we can each believe in our own power to become a light to another person, to be considered a gift to another soul. *Chaplains Walk*, the stories of her journey, will raise up every reader no matter their current disposition.

Marlene Capps MD MSHD CPE
Chief Medical Officer

Introduction

ILLNESS IS THE GREAT EQUALIZER. It is no respecter of age, gender, culture, or social status. Frequently leading to spiritual places of reckoning, illness and death hold no loyalties and show few mercies.

As a chaplain, I developed firsthand awareness of the effects of spiritual beliefs on medical treatment choices, recuperation, and coping skills. I learned the world's most prevalent religions engage in the utilization of spiritual support during illness and death, validated through ongoing patient, family, and spiritually proactive clinician support requests.

Although fluid, approximately eighty-four percent of the world's population professes religious affiliation (Pew Research Center Religion & Public Life Report, 2020), the type of which remains a personal choice in most, though not all, cultures. "Why Doctors Now Believe Faith Heals" (Washingtonian 2001) bridged the physician-chaplain relationship for me in early ministry, highlighting connections between health and faith often held by medical professionals. I learned longevity, shorter recovery, lower blood pressure and occurrence of coronary disease, better mental health, and reduced stress levels have proven links to faith. Interactions and observations throughout my career with physicians and patients solidified my belief that faith can and does influence health.

Hospital engagement of chaplain support is often based on approximations of religious populations. Community and volunteer clergy typically remain available to minister to patients whose specific religion may not be represented by staff chaplains. Hospital chaplains facilitate spiritual care in accordance with patient requirements and coordinate patient-family religious support with family clergy.

My personal theological beliefs are in Jesus Christ. While serving as a hospital chaplain, I assisted others in their personal theological journeys to the best of my ability, responding honestly to questions of spiritual exploration while providing support, compassion, and empathy—needs common to all. I believe it is our spiritual responsibility to uphold one another, to strengthen, comfort, and help as best we can as we journey through this world together.

Chaplain's Walk contains many accounts of personal spiritual journeys with my fellow explorers over the past twenty-five years. Attempting to capture these profound interactions, as *Chaplain's Walk* neared completion, experiences on a deeply personal level, including breast cancer, my father's suicide, and the death of my mother following her extended care, forged emotional yet hopeful final chapters.

My desire is first to glorify God as I have penned these sacred interactions in the ministry of a chaplain's walk. It is my sincere prayer that readers will be encouraged and strengthened in their own spiritual journeys—that loved ones, families, caregivers, hospital professionals, and fellow clergy may investigate the deep realms of spirituality to find peace and strength, and to know the pain of illness and death can bring about growth, and perception that this world is not all there is. The touching of our souls in this way may well be future conversations to be had, here and in Heaven, as God is with and in each one of us.

"Praise be to the Lord and Father of our Lord, Jesus Christ, the Father of compassion and God of all comfort, who comforts us in all our troubles, so that we can comfort those who are in any trouble, with the comfort we ourselves receive from God" (II Corinthians 1:3 & 4 NIV).

1

A Big Man

I am paged to the oncology unit. As I walk into the room, I see the patient is a big man; a big man with a big disease that is killing him. Soft music is coming from a CD player someone has placed on his bedside table. He looks at me and I tell him I am the hospital chaplain. "I just came by to check on you." He reaches out to shake my hand, but he does not release it.

He says, "I want to go home."

"I understand," I tell him. In the years to come, I will realize how little I knew.

He says his family has left for the night, and I see he is holding a small stuffed dog. I comment, and he replies, "The pup will make a good hunting dog." I ask if he hunts. "I went hunting for the first time with my dad when I was eight," he tells me. "My dad wouldn't give me a gun. He told me to follow close and be quiet. When we got done, I asked my dad if I did okay. He told me, 'You did good for an ole' boy.' Then I asked, 'How did I do for a man?' He said, 'You did good for an ole' boy.'" The big man smiles pensively, recalling these long-ago moments with his father.

The man speaks of World War II. "I've been in eleven battles," he tells me. "I didn't like shooting at people I couldn't see. I was never afraid after that first battle." The man has experienced much in his lifetime. He has traveled around the world nine times. I sense he is afraid of this battle. His brow is furrowed, determined. He knows he is dying. He is trying to remain courageous, trying to do good for an "ole boy."

I tell him how amazing his life sounds like it has been. He says, "Yeah, I've done a lot of things." I know he has never done anything like this. I want to tell him it will be okay, but those words would sound untrue. He has spent time facing the truth, and I want to respect that. I ask if he would like to pray. He nods his head, closing his eyes. I take his hand once more. God is familiar with him and knows far better than me the comfort this man needs. When our prayer has ended, I feel the sacred ground rising around us, becoming a part of his world travels. It upholds him, and I will keep a part of his journey as well. As I leave, my continued prayer is for this man to be able to hold onto the strength and dignity he so closely guards. More than this, when he enters Heaven, I am certain he will hear God say, "You did good for a man."

Sustaining the Spirit

The spirit in each of us is one of the most unique components of our being. You cannot touch it. Or can you? How important is the well-being of the spirit? Can the condition of the spirit cause us to live longer? Die sooner? Just as clinicians care for the body, the interlocking relationship between body and spirit recognized in patient care often requires spiritual treatment as well. During my career, it has routinely been my privilege to connect with individuals at an amazing point of their being known as the *human spirit.*

Empathy, listening, and encouragement all lead to spiritual strengthening. For members of the medical team, treatment is prescribed based on what is considered necessary to sustain and improve patient health. Chaplains assist the patient, family, and, at times, the medical team in seeking that which will sustain the spirit, and thereby the mind and body.

In the face of critical illness or impending death, what some view as *false hope,* others view as faith. Hope which sustains the spirit through one more day, one more hour, or one more minute, is anything but false. Spiritual strength for some includes the belief that if the medical battle is lost, the spiritual war is won by stepping through Heaven's gate. The apostle Paul declared, "Even if our earthly house is destroyed, we have a building from God . . . Eternal in the heavens" (II Corinthians, 5:1 NKJV).

Better is Always a Good Word

When inquiring how a patient is doing, I often hear, "I feel a little better today." This may be the result of care the patient has received since admission. Appropriate medical treatment can positively affect an individual's mental and emotional condition, resulting in a sense of well-being and awareness of feeling *better.* This explains comments of improvement from the sickest patients. It may be the pain has temporarily subsided, or the patient is able to hold down food for the first time in days, or simply that the patient is experiencing an emotional, mental, or spiritually *better* place since admission. Whatever the reason, the moment attests improvement, no matter how miniscule, and through this observance, I have come to understand, "better" is always a good word.

Because *better* often involves the spirit, it is at times the result of being heard. As the individual shares parts of his or her journey, this self-reflection may summon inner strength as being *listened to* releases affirmation. Though we do not have the answers for every search within the human spirit, *better* can occur when one is simply being acknowledged and valued.

2

The Need to Believe

Whether referred to as spiritual support, pastoral care, or organizational ministry, chaplaincy is ultimately the giving of compassion to another's spirit. The effects of spiritual care relating to health have been a part of healthcare in one form or another throughout recorded history. The human spirit bears *the need to believe* in something—to search for something in addition to medical facts. Focusing only on medical aspects can result in the loss of hope. Adding the strength of spiritual sustenance and the power of hope can assist in sustaining the spirit and may even change the outcome.

A socioeconomic decline of illness exists with better medical treatment, though the occurrence of illness and death often appear not to be respecters of *anything*. Higher incidence of specific diseases may be identified with culture, ethnicity, heredity, and lifestyle, though often identifying factors fail to produce concrete proof for critical illness onset. While medical dots at times connect, explanations are often scarce or non-existent regarding the underlying selectiveness of illness.

Illness and death are imminent in this world. Patient and family choices—what they look to, believe in, and hold close to cope with illness and death—should be acknowledged and respected by all whom embark upon this sacred journey with them. The healthcare team of physicians, nurses, social workers, palliative care, and chaplains, as well as a myriad of other specialties, seeks to provide integral treatment for the mind, body, and spirit of everyone placed in their charge.

Most humans minister through positive actions, shared thoughts and beliefs, and treatments rendered. To *minister* is, "To give service, care, or aid; attend, as to wants or necessities; to contribute, as to comfort or happiness" (Dictionary.com 2021). Ministry is *receiving* as well. Philip Kapleau observed, "As people wanting to help others, we have probably all had experiences where we have gained courage to face our own problems from the courage we have seen in the people we have been trying to help" (*The Wheel of Life and Death*, 1989).

Clinical pastoral education (CPE) equips chaplains to meet patients where they are in each circumstance. Members of healthcare ideally join with family to provide the understanding and support each patient requires. It takes a *team* to facilitate specialized medical treatment for the patient as well as support to his or her family. As a dance instructor once told me, "If you do not dance as a team, nothing else matters." Whether within hospital walls or one's family structure, formulating a team signifies working together to make appropriate choices, providing spiritual provision, and lending emotional and mental support, compassion, and empathy. Illness necessitates a time of coming together to uphold one another in a spirit of caring—the same spirit of caring which leads many individuals into healthcare, or into a family and friend circle of love, or both.

The Patient's Side of the World

The patient's perspective is often a menagerie of hope and despair, faith and disbelief. The patient and family frequently begin their journey by assessing what they know. "What has your physician told you?" I often ask. The medical groundwork can be built upon as other team members interact with the patient and family concerning spiritual needs, treatment choices, and if necessary, end-of-life decisions. Information provided by the physician serves as a foundation upon which other disciplines more easily introduce advance care planning, selection of healthcare agents, and code status. Multi-disciplinary team members can assist in formulating a care plan through shared facts and perspectives. This teamwork often results in understanding what it looks like from the patient's viewpoint, from his or her side of the world.

Chaplains provide support for patients and families working to process a range of emotions; sadness, shock, anger, despair, and challenges of faith and hope are common. Wherever those we accompany must go mentally, emotionally, and spiritually to cope with illness, we must go as well. I have said to patients, families, and staff, "I am here if you need to talk, pray, cry, or scream." This statement normalizes thoughts and emotions which may feel *anything but normal* and acknowledges we are all human beings striving to do the best we can with situations we never anticipated facing. A chaplain represents a safe place for people in distress to vent, question, challenge the fairness of life, and if need be, even the love of their God. Individuals need this space in time to process circumstances in a way which can strengthen and provide relief of a burden never meant to be carried alone.

No Words

"A voice was heard in Ramah, lamentation, weeping, and great mourning, Rachel weeping *for* her children, refusing to be comforted . . ." (Matthew 2:18 NKJV).

I am paged to the emergency department. The patient advocate on duty meets me crying outside the room where the patient is lying on a gurney. The medical team has been unable to resuscitate this patient, a small child. Her mother is standing beside her, holding her tiny hand. This little girl has been crushed underneath a dresser which toppled over while she was playing at the babysitter's. Her mother was called at work and directed to meet the ambulance at the hospital. This is where I enter . . . God in Heaven knows there are no words for this. I touch the mother softly on the small of her back. Although she looks at me, she is not present. The shock and horror of losing her child prevents her from feeling anything else in these awful moments. I look at this beautiful child, and choke on my own tears as I see her sweet curls, the chubbiness that makes a baby so precious, and the innocence which brought her here, a child at play.

Forever in my soul remains a peripheral memory. The best friend of the baby's mother arrives and stands beside her at the gurney. Because the mother has come from work, she has on the heels she wore this day. Her friend, kneeling down beside her, removes the shoes from the grief-stricken mother's feet, then gently replaces them with her own, a pair of softly worn flip flops. In her painful state, the mom hardly seems to notice, though this gesture of love will remain written in time. And while the physicians were unable to save this child, while neither the medical staff, nor patient advocate, and not even the chaplain could reach through this mother's grief, her friend knelt at her feet and became the hands of Christ.

3

"Do you See Heaven? Is it Beautiful?"

When we discover medical science cannot always heal, it is then that we often consider what is on the other side of Heaven. When we lose a loved one, the greatest solace may be in the hope we will again see, hold, and express our love to that individual. On earth, our Father's voice speaks through the mind and heart. When we reach Heaven, the Bible says we will see *face to face*; we will witness Heaven and understand fully those things we have only heard or read about. Will it be as my dad said, "Just like earth, only perfect?"

Familiarity is often comforting, as many would readily embrace. Seeing my friend who died following an aneurism walk up and place her hands on each side of my face, entering my personal space as only she could do, would be wonderful. Seeing my grandparents wave through the window of their kitchen door, welcoming me into the wood-stove-scented warmth of their presence, sounds like a great Heaven to me. But I am not there yet, and I can only imagine, as the hymn goes, "What is beyond Heaven's gate." If dying is Heaven, then as Paul declares, ". . . Mortality will be swallowed up by life" (II Corinthians 5:4 NKJV).

There are times the solidity we claim as faith struggles to carry us. When we are not able to see or feel the arms of God, when fate and longevity appear to spin on a dime, our great aspirations give way to the realities of our vulnerability. Illness and tragedy change our lives radically and, at times, suddenly. What awaits us if we or someone we love must leave our familiar existence? If *the sky is the limit* on earth, then what exists in Heaven? During years of considering this question, I developed a personal spiritual belief that in Heaven we will be set free to experience our optimal selves; to embrace a limitless life in a perfect place, where the streets just may be made of gold! "Eye has not seen, nor ear heard, nor have entered into the heart of man, the things which God has prepared for those who love Him" (I Corinthians 2:9).

If the most intelligent person taps into only a small percentage of his or her brain power, why do we have so much unused potential? Could it be we short-circuited ourselves in the beginning of creation? If God provided us with profound knowledge and free will, placing us on an optimal path in a perfect place, could we have misused those gifts thereby forfeiting perfection? Perhaps we will more than regain ourselves in Heaven, reaching our fullest potential. Perhaps God will cut us loose to create and discover things we only dreamt of on earth. Couple that with perfect peace and Heaven will reach beyond what we have imagined. Regardless, on this side of Heaven, we will continue to celebrate one another's triumphs and accompany each other through perils until we arise victorious to assemble in Heavenly places.

Hopefully, the idea of Heaven as a perfect sorrow-free, illness-free existence will one day be realized by us all. For now, those of us who are not critically ill will accompany those who are.

A doctor I have worked with for many years speaks softly to a dying patient who previously shared her faith and belief in a perfect life after this one. The woman stares into the distance, appearing to see something amazing which the physician is unable to see. The physician bends down close and gently whispers in her patient's ear, "Do you see Heaven? Is it beautiful?"

4

The Sacred Ground
of Nursing

A Study of Spirituality

The struggle to understand the atrocities of illness and death are perhaps no more evident than in the field of nursing. The empathy of this soulful profession is palpable at times as countless professional nurses address the wounds of the body, as well as those of the soul. My graduate research examined the vocation of nursing as a ministerial calling, as I sought to identify existing links between nursing and personal spiritual decision-making. Twenty RN/BSN participants representing a ten-year minimum work history in various positions and experiential expertise answered questions concerning vocational choice, connections between spirituality and nursing, awareness of spirituality upon professional responsibilities, effects of spirituality upon patient care over career course, and spirqualty related to professional success. This group of professionals, daily defining and fulfilling patient needs, stood highly qualified to address personal spirituality in clinical patient care.

Research showed formations of bonding through mutually shared experience in the nursing community. The broader basis of why nurses enter this regimented program revealed contemplation frequently inspired by personal experience, often when young, and most recounted a specific experience or relationship which determined, at least in part, the pursuit of a nursing profession.

Study participants included first to third generation US citizens and first to second generations originally hailing from abroad, providing a strong multi-cultural characterization. Alphabetically, African, American, Eastern European (Serbian), Filipino, French, German, Greek, Icelandic, Irish, Italian, Scottish, Swedish, and Welch nationalities were represented.

Study Results

Many participants claimed a dependence upon his or her spirituality in providing daily care for their patients, though the majority did not equate the choice of a nursing career with spiritual decision-making connected to religion. Although nursing as a profession was not proven to be solely linked to a spiritual calling, it *was* shown to have a connection to personal spiritual decision-making. The study revealed the decision to become a nurse, though not necessarily a calling of the Holy Spirit (S), is often intertwined with the nurse's inner spirit (s), as the choice of a nursing profession easily blends with personal spiritual goals and convictions. One nurse stated, "I never felt my spirituality guaranteed me success but rather the strength to keep going."

Participants viewed education as preparatory opportunity to serve humankind. Excelling in their fields and often transcending to supervisory roles, the majority indicated leading with their hearts, and most emphasized a personal experience or influence salient in choosing a profession of caring for others. Study results revealed long-running cohesiveness among participants. "A test of peoples groupness is durability; that is, a group's identity and allegiance must remain over time" (Bennett & Felder 2003).

Common themes of kindness and compassion, depth and spiritual awareness, as well as meaningful conviction of purpose were reflected by participant input. Individuals evidenced a common vision of serving others in need. "Members act in concert because they share a common organizational vision and understand how their own work helps build on that shared vision" (Eisenberg, et al, 2010). Fulfilling patient needs fulfills the nurses' need to care. These amazing individuals not only serve professionally, but often as a family hub of medical information and support. Guiding other nurses, healthcare professionals, and at times physicians, each one purported to be inspired by and rely upon a personal inner strength.

Illness and death affect patients and families every day in unimaginable ways as nurses continue to provide medical treatment while extending mental, emotional, and often spiritual support. At the heart of each nurse exists a selfless, driven spirit dedicated to the care and compassion involved in the support of humankind. My research data revealed nurses offer both patients and families a safe place to voice thoughts, fears, hopes, and even questions on life and faith.

In the hospital setting, events occur that one can never understand on this side of Heaven. Illnesses ravage, lives end, consequences of lifestyles and rash decisions surface, unanticipated diagnoses are delivered, and the atrocities of abuse and harm are witnessed. The heartbreaking unfairness of childhood diseases are among the battles waged by patients housed within hospital walls. At the bedside stands an individual adorned by angel wings and armor, on vigilant watch, administering brief freedoms through medications, as well as hope and healing through treatments which assuage and remedy. And the reasons these individuals stand guard—the beacon calling them to the bedside—is what each nurse perceives to be the center of their being, the spirit beckoning each of them to wage a battle, not on his or her own behalf, but rather on the behalf of another. Perhaps the most important thing the nurse gives is his or her presence as the feelings, attitudes, strengths, failures, and successes involved in the struggle of the human spirit in coping with illness are affirmed by the great heart and spirit of the professional nurse.

Diagnosed with Multiple Sclerosis, one nurse whom I had the privilege to work with stoically stated, "For now I stand on this side of the bed . . ." Life is fragile. We do not always know what path our journey upon this earth will take. And the element of mystery for us remains; we are often strengthened by those things which demand the most of who we are and choose to be.

Patient Expectations and Nursing

Many challenges face the fast-paced, ever-changing world of healthcare, as the medical community remains consistently involved in the ongoing examination of patient needs and expectations, as well as provisions offered by the healthcare industry. The impact of spirituality upon the human condition is routinely observed by lifeline professionals who play an integral part in patient care from birth to death. Press Ganey research reveals, "Patients place a high value on their emotional and spiritual needs" (2002). "Studies have found a strong positive relationship between spirituality/religiosity and health and well-being" (*American Society of Registered Nurses*, 2017).

Identifying *holistic* healthcare, a clinical term inclusive of spiritual support, T. E. Johnston observed, "Prayer is a normal spiritual expression of approximately 9 out of 10 individuals, with health or health issues a common topic" (*Focus on Spirituality in Nursing Intervention*, 2003). Johnston looks at whether this regularly utilized component of spirituality is expected by the patient and family to be an element of nursing care, suggesting most individuals incorporate prayer into their spiritual and physical health concerns. Johnston acknowledges the benefits of interactive prayer, often with nurses: "Because prayer frequently sustains coping and brings comfort, it is an important resource for nurses to support or offer." According to Johnston, this improves coping skills and often the overall health of the patient, though he advocates discernment in determining which patients desire prayer as part of their holistic health care treatment. I have learned prayer should be offered in a manner which the patient feels comfortable declining as well.

Nurses take their jobs personally as an element of intimacy exists in administering care ranging from non-urgent to intensive critical care. Unable to anticipate the situation, they do anticipate their involvement in treating the patient in his or her entirety of mind, body, and spirit. Reinert and Koenig go as far as defining all interactions between nurse and patient as "spiritual," depending upon one's definition of the word ("Re-examining Definitions of Spirituality in Nursing Research," *JAN* 2013). This concept reveals the gray area of spirituality in nursing, in contrast to other spiritual ministries.

The following reflections of a retired nurse concluded my research: "Nurses are the heroes and heroines of the medical profession. Who else is routinely exposed to the lusty wail of a newborn, or privy to a patient's smile when walking for the first time following joint replacement? Who holds the hand of a cardiac patient in the midnight hour? Woven into the medicinal tapestry, always, is a nurse working long hard hours, returning home often to care for a family. So, the next time a nurse cares for you, be sure to say, 'Thank you for all you have been called to do'" (Simonds, 2014). Thank you, Mom, for the fifty years you gave your patients and family.

The continual journey of medical research attests to a never-ending quest to heal and prolong life, as perhaps in no other profession is suffering examined more closely than healthcare. As illness besets patient and family, those who accept the charge of caring for them stand courageously through heartbreak and hope. *Thank you* to all the heroines and heroes in the nursing field.

5

Continue . . .

Chaplaincy routinely involves offering spiritual support to individuals one has never met prior to his or her hospitalization. In contrast, when spiritual support involves friends or family, unique challenges arise. When my mother was diagnosed with endometrial cancer, I struggled with how I might best support her. Familiar with the components of providing spiritual services in a professional setting, ministering in a personal family relationship added a different element. For clergy, the desire to minister perfectly to those we love can result in discovering ourselves lost in the attempt.

Chaplain education teaches the objectivity necessary in learning one cannot *fix* the illness, though the desire to make it alright when it is not alright can be especially overwhelming during spiritual interactions with close friends or family. As I witnessed my mother's vulnerability, my emotions affected knowledge previously accrued in studying religion and gained through experience. When feelings of inadequacy surfaced and various thoughts of what I might do or say seemed *not enough,* I feel at a loss, emotionally and mentally overwhelmed. I learned if I continued doing what I knew, asking what she needed from me, I was a good spiritual support person for her, and more importantly, a supportive daughter.

My mother, small in stature, feisty in spirit, and deeply religious, remained physically beautiful throughout her life. Affectionate displays were not her forte, though intelligence and femininity were. Completing an education in nursing as a young woman, she worked in the field until retirement at seventy-two. Requested and loved by patients as well as the physician for whom she worked, when attempting to retire (several times), mom's doc would *up the ante*. It became a joke between them when she approached him with retirement plans, as he would simply ask, "How much do you need [to stay]?"

Following Mom's cancer diagnosis, one word often drifted through my heart: "Continue." Derived from its simplicity, the word provided comfort for her as well as for me. *Continue* applies to who we are, what we believe, and where we are going. Possessing no great challenge other than not giving up, *continue* applies to the present as well as to eternity, to those who are ill, and to those who love them.

I learned the difficulties in squaring my profession with a strong desire to provide effective ministry in a personal relationship. I came to understand passionate professionals should perhaps not attempt to separate out professional choices or callings from the persons they are. Since this intertwining is often so strong, whether in ministry, medicine, or any other heartfelt vocation, the attempted separation can cause confusion and emotional turmoil. Better to be left whole!

Living ten hours apart, we often sent my parents greeting cards between calls and visits to express our love and support. Ironically, following mom's hysterectomy, I found a card bearing the silhouette of a woman which inside simply read, "Continue . . ." God is good.

6

Without Understanding

I walk into a room where the patient and family not only desire answers, but they also expect their spiritual support person to provide them. "Why?" is a recurring question, though often there is no answer. Frequently, explanations are not possible with serious illnesses and injuries. Difficult to understand or accept, the patient and family often desire to make sense of the situation. I can only provide support for the exploration, believing what one cannot make sense *of,* faith will make possible to cope *with.*

What was it that caused the forty-three-year-old patient in ICU to sit down to breakfast with his wife and collapse with a brain bleed? No family history of stroke, no personal history of drug or alcohol abuse; he never even smoked a cigarette. When stressors are considered, his lifestyle reflects nothing unusual. By accounts, he is happy in his personal life and satisfied with his vocation, absent undue stressors. If we could at least make one explanation fit, we might make some sense of it all, but the truth is, we cannot. It is inexplicable.

In the next room lies an individual who has led a self-debilitating life. Do we find it less disturbing to accept his dilemma because of the need to see life play out fairly? We must often give up understanding "why," as we walk by faith. I fulfil my calling as a hospital chaplain without having all the answers, though the inability to square life with justice is a shared struggle most hospital disciplines face daily.

I sit at a conference table full of highly qualified nurse managers and charge nurses representing each hospital unit. They discuss our patient who has lost the ability to speak, as well as right-side movement. We have come alongside him and his wife and confer how to best provide exemplary care to this patient and family, which includes three children under five years of age. These critical care nurses, elite providers of core needs for body, mind, and spirit, do not attempt to explain the injustice of the situation, though it is in our consciences. Rather, they offer compassion of the deepest kind—accompaniment on a journey with those for whom there exists no answer to, "Why?"

Acutely aware of the expertise around this table, it has been my privilege to share years and countless moments with these same nurses in patient rooms. I have provided support to them during their own personal challenges. Though I speak words of encouragement during staff meetings, it is not my desire to offer spiritually pat answers to experts hailing from over-censused short-staffed units. Following patient updates, one nurse asks about my mom's health, and I receive support back from those God has placed in my path. As they speak of patients, families, and of their own families, we briefly discuss the injustices of illness. I have chosen a reading from Greg Yoder's *Companioning the Dying*:

> "'Why did God choose me for this disease?' . . . I was sitting by this young woman, barely forty years old, who was dying. As she continued to stare into space, I noticed my mind scanning for an immediate list of possible responses. My index included, 'Oh, Dora, I don't think God chose you for this disease. It's nobody's fault.' Next was, 'Perhaps you're a person who has more courage to

endure this than others.' My silent responses began sounding more absurd: 'I don't know, but maybe this is an opportunity to learn some important things you're supposed to learn.' I could see this was going nowhere fast . . .

I was amazed at how quickly my mind ran amok. Our conditioning to make people feel better by offering quick explanations and solutions is deeply rooted. Sometimes it takes great discipline for me to remain silent during moments like that.

As I watched her eyes, I found the good sense to just quietly hold with her the immensity of the question. She was engaged inside herself, searching for a context in which to bear this horrible thing she could not stop. But this important work belonged to her . . .

Those facing death as well as their loved ones may question familiar philosophical and spiritual values or suddenly revisit dormant religious roots. When I observe the dying painfully struggling for meaning, I am deeply touched and inspired. I often tell them, 'This search for meaning is such an important thing . . . What a struggle to be engaged in . . . You can count on me to walk with you'" (Yoder, 2015).

I look up from the reading to see somber faces, a sense of community and understanding, even relief. As their chaplain and support person, we share the knowledge it is *painful* not to have answers. I know they see ungodly things, perhaps more than me. But our souls search for enough of God's grace to enable us to be with those for whom we often cannot provide answers. God's love is manifest in presence, and even in helplessness.

As we exit the meeting, one of the nurses catches me. "My mother had uterine cancer a year ago," she says. "She's doing great and is cancer free." We discuss our moms' medical histories. I am strengthened and comforted by additional medical information she offers. I walk away thinking how God makes His presence known; so precise is His timing, assisting us in upholding one another. I am honored to be given the opportunity once again to share time with these nurses, holding in my soul utmost respect.

My mind drifts back to the patient upstairs, his wife constantly by his side. I think how blessed he is by those who surround his bed.

"When we honestly ask ourselves which persons in our lives mean most to us, we often find it is those who . . . have chosen to share our pain with a gentle and tender hand. The friend who can be silent with us in a moment of despair . . . who can stay with us in an hour of grief . . . who can tolerate not knowing . . . not healing, and face with us the reality of our powerlessness . . ." (Nouwen, 1974).

7

Denominational Diversity

What God represents to one individual may seem foreign to another. Though diverse, I have observed most religious and theological values include a place of safety or refuge where the patient and family may find rest and replenishment for their bodies as well as their souls.

In addition to medical treatment, patients and families seek mental, emotional, and spiritual strength to cope with illness as well as continuing responsibilities. While illness brings stressors, the demands of life continue whether the patient is able to or not. The patient and family will hold to spiritual beliefs which strengthen and comfort them, often praying for healing while preparing for anything which lies ahead. This strengthening includes their God and the belief system associated with their God.

A Measure of Faith and Diversity

The apostle Paul speaks of human diversity, gifts, relationships, and humility. Culture, background, and beliefs illuminate our lives with differences, as scripture points to the beauty and usefulness of differences, as well as commonalities. Consider Paul's advice which remains significant in our present diverse society.

> "For I say, through the grace given to me, to everyone who is among you, not to think of himself more highly than he ought to think, but to think soberly, as God has dealt to each one a measure of faith. For as we have many members in one body, but all the members do not have the same function, so we being many are one body in Christ and individually members of one another. Having then gifts differing according to the grace that is given to us, let us use them: if prophecy, let us prophesy in proportion to our faith; or ministry, let us use it in our ministering; he who teaches, in teaching; he who exhorts, in exhortation; he who gives, with liberality; he who leads, with diligence; he who shows mercy, with cheerfulness" (Romans 12:3-8 NKJV).

> "Let love be without hypocrisy. Abhor what is evil. Cling to what is good. Be kindly affectionate to one another with brotherly love, in honor giving preference to one another, not lagging in diligence, fervent in spirit, serving the Lord; rejoicing in hope, patient in tribulation, continuing steadfastly in prayer . . . given to hospitality. . . Rejoice with those who rejoice, and weep with those who weep. Be of the same mind toward one another. Do not set your mind on high things but associate with the humble. Do not be wise in your own opinion. Repay no one evil for evil. Have regard for good things in the sight of all men. *If it is possible, as much as depends on you, live peaceably with all men*" (Romans 12:9-17, selected verses, italics added for emphasis).

Humor in Diversity

A maximum census has caused the telemetry unit to double up in certain rooms, and I discover my referral has a roommate. Both female patients have improved from initial diagnoses of chest pain. Each in her sixties, from different cultural and ethnic backgrounds, one Greek Orthodox, one Baptist. The first lady recounts her experience of chest pain at work, following a co-worker's advice to get to the hospital. She speaks of her faith and expresses hope she will be alright.

The second patient joins the conversation, sharing her own frightening experience and thankfulness for timely treatment. The conversation takes a turn when she unabashedly states she sucks her thumb at night to get to sleep. The tele-roommate stares at her in disbelief, though this does not deter the thumb-sucker as she laughingly shares that she often stays awake *all night*. This elicits an eye-roll from her roommate which I pretend not to notice, making a mental note to ask the night nurse to monitor the situation. Following our chat, we pray. *Two individuals with similar medical needs and diverse personalities, relying upon the same God.* His power unites them in a place of familiarity with one another in spirit, no matter the differences. I thank God for an evening of diversity and unity, along with the ability to smile.

8

Recognizing God's Voice

A young child of seven hears God call early in the night. Climbing out of bed, she goes to find her mother, telling her of hearing God's voice. Her mother leads the child to the nearby bathroom where they kneel beside the tub as the child asks Christ into her heart. Though they have never prayed in the bathroom, this significance will later become clear.

"Do You Remember Me?"

A young woman senses what can only be described as God's close, constant presence. One night as she bathes, she bows her head, "God, what is it you want from me?" The Holy Spirit within her immediately attests to the ministerial call upon her life. Filled with humility, the awareness of *everything she is not* floods her mind, as she asks, "God, do you remember me?" His message permeates her heart, and she can only weep.

For weeks, she discusses her calling only with God, eventually sharing with those closest to her. The young woman's pastor is affirming, encouraging her to explore and pursue God's direction. Her maternal grandmother, spiritual teacher and guide, places her hands on each side of the young woman's shoulders. "I believe you will make a wonderful minister, Janny."

Each ministerial calling has its own unfolding, and this was mine. It is my belief God communicates with each person in a manner which will enable him or her to understand the call. Our free will determines the answer, though God provides the courage needed to accept it. My pastor once told me, "Callings do not disappear; even if we *never* answer them." I also learned, stepping into a calling is not a race, but a *life-long journey*. Even the educational pieces, while important, are not an end-all, and experience remains a vital learning curve in ministry.

Ministry does not require perfection. As a chaplain with personal flaws, past mistakes, and weaknesses, it took me time to understand it was partially *because* of these things that God called. Regardless of personal spiritual beliefs, humankind remains imperfect, and the same is true for those called to minister. Through faith in Christ, there is forgiveness as His crucifixion and resurrection gives us new life. God created us because he *wanted* to, and though we many times turn away, He sets us free from the bondage of sin, guilt, and shame. "Though your sins be as scarlet, they shall be as white as snow" (Isaiah 1:18 KJV).

Depending upon church and family for spiritual guidance, I anticipated a ministerial path would bring challenges. They appeared quickly when my mother was not initially supportive. "Jan," she offered, "I never believed women should fulfil pastoral positions in the church," citing Paul's direction concerning the impropriety of a woman speaking in church. Though well-meaning, even those close to us may deter our spirit. Every calling includes the responsibility to search for clarity. My mother eventually gave her support, overcoming misconstrued views on the developed role of women in the church. Holding to the source of my call for strength and direction, I watched as each roadblock fell away or was conquered. "If God is for us, who can be against us?" (Romans 8:31 NIV).

Inspiration filled my heart as sermons played like recordings in my mind from start to finish, invocation to benediction. I assumed a future in church ministry, though God often has plans for us we cannot anticipate. He knows our niches. I accepted an invitation from my pastor to speak before the congregation on a Good Friday, facing down anxieties and accepting the invitation as an act of faith and obedience as Christ's servant. Over the years, God taught me to trust more in Him and less in feelings of anxiety or self-doubt. I learned if my goal was to glorify God, everything else would fall into place.

While finishing a BS in Christian ministry, I began working in ministry part-time, later completing a residency in clinical pastoral education (CPE), and an MA in ministerial leadership. After working two years in a skilled nursing facility and the church, ultimately God led me to the hospital setting. Years earlier, I attended nursing school at the prompting of my parents, completing two years of the three-year program when I realized this was *their* dream, not mine. That education, however, served me well in hospital chaplaincy as I was able to understand many clinical aspects pertaining to the patients to whom I ministered.

The calling upon our lives is never limited to one purpose. My pastor was correct; a ministerial calling never goes away. It continues and changes and the recipient of the call continues to grow during this ebb and flow. I learned, w*hen I allow God to remain in control of my direction, my flaws will not cause me to fail.* It is only when I take charge that I become uncertain. Perfection is not a requirement in ministry, but a willingness to persevere is.

I came to understand the meaning of a child kneeling beside a bathtub receiving Christ, and a young woman called to ministry while bathing. I grew to embrace these aqueous places of spiritual encounter. We were created with nothing between us and our Creator, as there was again nothing between God and me when He called me to minister. There I encountered His direction, and the washing away *of all I was not.* In these spiritual places, I chose to trust God with whom I was and could ever be through His grace.

Ministerial Comedy

A minister walks through his front door with a parrot on his shoulder. His surprised wife asks, "Where in the world did you get that thing?"

The parrot replies, "At the church!"

9

"Company Always Makes the Coffee Taste Sweeter!"

I have just begun part-time work as a chaplain in a skilled nursing facility while finishing an undergraduate degree. I wonder, "What could I possibly have to teach these men and women?" What I do not understand, what I cannot yet know, is that God has not sent me to teach them. He has sent me to *learn* from them. In this thirty-seven-bed facility, I am to witness many things regarding aging, wisdom, and the human spirit.

Following one Sunday worship service, I sit with a female resident, a tiny, spry, long-time SNF dweller. "May I sit with you?" I ask.

"Why yes," she replies with a smile. "Company always makes the coffee taste sweeter, you know!" I will come to cherish these faces and personalities as they teach me of their strength, resilience, humor, and tenacity. And most of all, they will teach me of their faith.

Skilled nursing facilities essentially contain an entire world for the elderly. Just as we live within the confines of our home, community, and globe, nursing facilities define the parameters for residents. As with ours, their world is ever-changing. Residents are naturally vulnerable through circumstance, as age and health create an ebb and flow which is often challenging for residents as well as staff. Maintaining positivity is crucial, yet there are strong forces at work within these mini worlds. Aging often prevents spontaneity and venturing beyond their walls requires careful planning. Unlike the outside world, residents live in a limited environment, unable to enjoy many freedoms we take for granted.

SNF residents are often beset by widescale ailments from arthritis to dementia. I observe that residents who appear to fare best mentally and emotionally are those who remain flexible in their acceptance of circumstances. Residents who defiantly struggle against aging and the necessity of dependence upon others are more susceptible to discontent or anger, often focused on what they perceive to be a sense of weakness or helplessness. My time at the SNF teaches me those who appear happier have come to accept this season in life. Residents who are more accepting of age and circumstance are statistically more content and can appreciate there are positive things about growing older. "Even to your old age and gray hairs, I am He, I am He who sustains you" (Isaiah 46:4 NIV). I am in awe of those who have embraced or accepted this time, the joy they seem to derive from each day and share with others. Whether enjoyment comes from receiving mail, visitors, or participating in small activities, they focus largely on the positive. We should be willing to do our share in the responsibility to our seniors to lighten their load in any way, large or small. Whenever possible, every elderly person should be precious to someone.

During a college assignment, I conduct a survey at the SNF comprised of simple ratings concerning perceptions related to care. Residents are asked to number topics in order of what they view as most important, and those needing assistance are helped by other residents or staff members. Items listed are (1) Nutritious meals, (2) Hot meals, (3) Medications on time, (4) Assistance with hygiene, (5) Physical therapy, (6) In-house Activities, (7) Receiving visitors, (8) Kindness from staff, (9) Receiving correspondence, and (10) Outings and trips. The results indicate the number one item of importance to them, without exception, is *kindness from the staff.* Never underestimate the power of kindness, especially for those whose resources to find it are limited.

The SNF Capers

Enjoying my work at the nursing facility, I become increasingly fond of the residents. Visiting a dementia patient who is Catholic, she asks to pray the Lord's Prayer. I kneel in front of her wheelchair as she takes my hand. As we finish, I prepare to stand when this tiny lady plants a left hook squarely in my eye. Luckily, the ophthalmologist is a few short blocks away. I come away with a corneal contusion and a shiner, plus a huge lesson on prayer positioning in the dementia unit. My supervisor knowingly advises, "Always kneel to the side."

Conducting Sunday services in addition to providing spiritual support, I routinely fashion humor into the sermons which helps keep residents alert. Keeping services brief and conducting them quickly at a slightly accelerated volume prevents them from snoozing. In summary, I've learned to hit 'em fast and hard! Residents have taught me humor remains a strength throughout life, as they always appreciate receiving or giving a smile. One gentleman tells me a joke and when I laugh, he says, "Good, I wanted to be sure. I told it during activity hour but half of 'em didn't get it, and the other half couldn't hear me!"

I encourage my children, ranging in age from elementary to middle school, to assist me by handing out programs and chatting with residents during coffee socials after church services. Interesting moments are never-ending. One little lady who often mistakes my ten-year-old daughter for a boy she calls *Danny,* says to my daughter, "You're a good boy, Danny!" While perplexing my young daughter, this delights her older sister.

At the time, it is considered cool in adolescent circles to wear *untied* shoelaces, and my ten-year-old attends services without tying her laces. One resident appears mesmerized by this, staring at my daughter's feet throughout the service and afterwards asks, "Why are your shoes untied? Why don't you tie your shoes?" I recognize my daughter's annoyance, once again to the delight of her older sister whom I am unsure finds these situations more humorous because of the resident's question or because of her curiosity in anticipating her younger sister's reaction. I smile at the patience my little daughter exhibits with only a fleeting roll of the eyes she thinks I do not notice.

My son is five and habitually sits by his favorite sweet, white-haired lady during Sunday services who happens to have dementia. Always, they share the *same* conversation:

(Resident) "What's *your* name?"
(My son tells her his name).
"You seem like a nice boy."
"Thank you."
She nods toward me. "Is that your mother?"
"Yes ma'am."
30-secound pause . . .
"What's *your* name?"
(My son again answers).
"You seem like a nice boy."
"Thank you."
"Is that your mother?" (Nodding toward me).
"Yes ma'am."

The conversation sometimes continues from the end of the service until we leave the facility, though my son is tireless in patiently answering his friend.

One female resident is 103 years old. In her younger years, I am told she was a talented concert pianist. Now largely non-verbal, she possesses a mischievous spirit. Quite adept at maneuvering her wheelchair, she finds it amusing to race in front of the other residents. As one gentleman slowly makes his way to the bathroom with his walker, she revs up her wheels, and before staff can make a move, she plows into the back of his knees. Barely reaching him in time, a male nursing assistant makes a good save. The gentleman, normally quiet, lumbers around to stare down his assailant, shaking his fist in the air shouting, "If you do that again, I'll pop you one!" After recounting the story to my kids, the phrase becomes one of our fondly used declarations.

The century-plus resident is also intrigued with my young son's Pokémon cards. He shows her each card as she looks and nods her approval. Occasionally, there is a card she does not like, and she shakes her boney fist. As my son goes through the deck during one visit, she says something we cannot understand and reaches out to strike him. Luckily for him, she is frail and fails to land the blow soundly. The event and surprised look on my son's face cause everyone nearby to share his wide-eyed expression followed by laughter we cannot contain. My son has just learned, *stand to the side* applies to prayer *and* Pokémon cards!

Romance never fizzles out in the human spirit. I observe a rather dapper elderly gentleman whose company the ladies seem to enjoy, and at times, compete for. Nothing about growing older stops the enjoyment of flirtation as the ladies vie for this gentleman's attention, especially during Bingo and activity hour. At one point, I intervene to interject a bit of *relationship empathy* as one pretty lady is sad her handsome friend has chosen another as his game partner. "No one could compete with your face," I tell her. Soon, she is smiling again. And she beats them!

The SNF utilizes a six-bed ward for male residents requiring an elevated level of care and supervision. RN's take rotations for this unit every seven days, and one nurse is pregnant and nearing her delivery date. Visiting this ward regularly, I have become familiar with the residents. One gentleman experiencing advanced Alzheimer's is convinced the nurse's baby belonged to another elderly resident in the ward who is largely immobile and practically comatose. I spend time assuring my distressed friend this is not the case. "Oh yes!" He insists of his bed-ridden ward-mate, "Wild things go on here at night! I could be like that if I wanted, but I don't." It is difficult to maintain a serious face during some of his descriptive tales. After the baby comes, the staff is happy the resident refocuses and begins sharing stories of his friendship with Bonnie and Clyde. *Much* tamer!

Throughout the years, skilled nursing facilities have utilized various communication techniques regarding dementia or Alzheimer residents. One tool encourages staff to help the resident *center*, using verbal reminders of reality. Since SNF's encounter various levels of these diagnoses, excessive reminders can produce frustration or agitation for some residents. An alternative method involves staff's entry into the resident's realm of reality. It is not so difficult, and pretending green beans are magically fun is much easier than attempting to educate a dementia patient on nutrition. Altered mental status will not prevent staff from providing quality care, as the goal is to help residents remain as present as possible without unnecessary stressors or medications.

During my work at the SNF, I encounter a visiting Lutheran pastor, the head chaplain of a small community hospital. He asks if I would consider part time work at the hospital. Though I initially decline the offer, I am unable to sleep and decide to pray about it (what a novel idea). I accept the position and consider God could be opening a door I did not anticipate. This is where my hospital chaplaincy career begins.

SNF Joke of the day

A doctor making rounds at a skilled nursing facility examines a senior gentleman complaining of a chronic pain in his leg. "I am afraid it is simply old age," the physician tells him. "There is nothing I can do."

"That can't be!" fumes the man. "You are a terrible doctor!"

"Why would you think so?" Asks the doctor.

"It's obvious!" The old gentleman snorts. "My other leg is fine, and it's the exact same age!"

The Sheriff

Visiting a loved one in the nursing home after having known them in their *former life* can seem surreal. Forever etched in my heart is the first visit my twelve-year-old daughter and I made to see my beloved grandfather when he was a nursing home resident. The gentleman we had known and loved all our lives had lived part of his lifetime prior to our existence. We felt we knew some of that life from the stories he shared. As deputy sheriff of his small southern town, he did not tolerate true crime. However, rumor had it that on occasion he allowed inebriated folk to spend a few hours in jail sobering up, offering them a hot meal, especially on a cold night. This could have been in part because Papa was a high functioning alcoholic himself. When I was a baby, which would have put him around forty, Granny told me Papa came home, told her he would never take another drink, and never did. My grandfather swore there was no such thing as an alcoholic, that each of us determines what strongholds we surrender to, and the ones we will not.

My grandfather's pale blue eyes sparkled with memory as he told stories from the past. He kept a large butcher knife with a dark wooden handle in a kitchen drawer, and on occasion recounted how, as deputy sheriff, he and a physician friend went to a home in response to a domestic dispute. Ride-a-longs back then were good company. When they arrived, out came a woman wielding the now infamous butcher knife, and my grandfather told how he had to *wrestle* it away from her. From his account, it was not an easy task, although all turned out well with everyone safe, including the woman. In jail, but safe! That was one of my favorite stories.

My grandparents lived in the country long before technology brought computers or cell phones. As Granny told it, they had fun playing games and finding things to entertain themselves. Papa told of his escapades in taking a run and jumping over the end of his and Granny's big four-poster bed. He said he would grab the horizontal post at the bottom and jump through his arms onto the bed. On one occasion, as he jumped, he accidentally cut both wrists with his toenails! Papa said what upset him most was to risk life and limb daily as deputy sheriff, then to nearly commit harikari with his own toenails!

When I was small, Papa and Granny added a twin poster bed to their bedroom which was supposed to be for me, though eventually Granny and I laid claim to the full poster bed while Papa slept in the smaller one. My grandfather talked in his sleep, and for me as a child, this was immensely entertaining. If he fell sleep first, Papa would inevitably begin talking. This grew to become a familiar, even comforting part of our bedtime routine.

I learned from my grandmother to say, "Be quiet, Papa," if his talking continued too late.

Papa would reply, "Yep," followed by a brief silence until he began sleep-talking once more. As I grew older and less entertained, I would go to bed earlier, trying to get to sleep before Papa went to bed and began talking.

My grandmother told me when they were a young married couple, in addition to sleep-talking, my grandfather would sometimes walk in his sleep. Papa came from a large family—eight brothers who were mostly all sleepwalkers and talkers. According to my great grandmother, *sleep-singers* even! Papa's mother spoke of the boys' sleep-singing, even *harmonizing* as they slept.

When my grandparents married, Granny said although he lost his singing group, Papa made up for it with frequent antics in the night. According to her, Papa would sometimes climb out of bed, asleep, get completely dressed, including his dress shirt, jacket, and bowtie, and go outside. For some reason, he never put socks or shoes on when sleep walking, so when his feet hit the cold grass, he woke up. At times, Granny would not realize he had gotten out of bed until she heard him coming back in, getting undressed, and using choice words to describe his frustration!

One of my grandparents most outlandish adventures involved news of a hotel fire in Atlanta. Initially hearing of this terrible event on the radio, my grandmother became fretful. When Papa came home from the sheriff's department, Granny informed him she tied several sheets together to help them escape their three-story white wood frame home in the event of a fire. Since their bedroom was on the top floor, my grandmother was now adamant regarding an escape plan. Knowing my grandfather's normally easy-going manner, I am quite sure he smiled and agreed to allay Granny's concerns. According to her, at some point that night, Papa sat up in bed suddenly, yelling, "Fire! Fire!" My grandmother was terrified, right up until she heard Papa's instructions, "Hang to my shirttail, and I'll carry you to safety!" They never told me what happened next, but I do not think it involved hanging from a shirttail!

My mother shared that the best time of her life as a child was when my grandfather was deputy sheriff of their small town. She said she loved riding her bike around town where everyone knew everyone, referring to her childhood as a "charmed existence."

I share this story of the person my grandfather was, the bold sheriff, loving father, grandfather, storyteller, gardener (he grew the biggest green beans in the South), and strong Christian, as these characteristics and accomplishments were not reflected in the skilled nursing facility where he came to reside at ninety-two. Those who cared for the fragile body of bent bones, wrinkled skin, and vague smile missed the joy in knowing the whole story. When my daughter and I visited, we expressed our love for him every bit as much as we always had, but he was ready to go! He *did not want* to hang out here, and when Granny beat him to Heaven, he followed close behind.

We will one day again see my precious grandparents waving hello from their kitchen door. To me, that is the perfect welcoming as I enter Heaven. I have come to believe *everyone we know or love who goes before us makes Heaven more familiar to us.* I believe this is God's wonderful and loving plan, and that even Heaven needs an honorable deputy sheriff . . .

10

Deep Places

I am a chaplain resident working evenings and the emergency department is full. Several patients have been admitted and moved to an area reserved for overflow, separated by curtains. As I round to check on them, one patient I estimate to be in her thirties engages me in conversation. She states she has had a "bad" day and drove herself to the hospital. We chat for a while regarding her battles with depression and the suicidal thoughts she has previously shared with the triage nurse. As I prepare to go, the patient motions me back to the bedside. I wait for her to speak as she suddenly grabs the front of my shirt, pulling me down so our faces are only a couple of inches apart. She whispers, "I won't hurt you."

Looking into her eyes, I reply, "I know." After a few seconds which seem longer, she releases her hold and I straighten up. "Are you alright?" I ask. "Would you like your nurse?"

"Can you get her?" She asks. "I'm not feeling well."

I assure her I will. I find her nurse right away, informing her of the event. The physician prioritizes a STAT psych eval, and security arrives to inform the patient she cannot touch staff in a threatening manner. Our T's are crossed, and the patient is in good hands. And I leave, a much wiser chaplain.

Deeper Places

Soft grievous weeping is audible behind the ED curtains. I gently separate them to find a woman, perhaps in her forties, standing beside the patient. She bends over him, resting her head on his chest. I quietly introduce myself and she asks, "Please pray for my father." She tells me he has suffered an aneurism and remains unresponsive. She is now awaiting test results for brain activity, prognosis, and a suggested medical path. The staff has prepared her for difficult news, and she believes it is coming. Together we pray for a miracle. Looking at me with swollen red eyes, she says, "My father has never given his life to Christ. I'm devastated. I feel I've let him down and my heart is broken thinking we can't be together in Heaven."

I tell her, "I believe God appeals to us through many people and experiences, and it is up to each individual whether to accept him. The responsibility to share God's love with your father did not rest solely upon one person, so be gracious to yourself." The daughter nods her head and begins to cry once more. The young chaplain in me wants to fix her pain, and I offer, "I like to believe somewhere in the recesses of an unconscious mind God is still able to reach us. It's possible your father has given his life to Christ."

Looking me in the eyes, she calmly says, "I don't know what Bible you read, but the one I read says my father is going to hell." This was perhaps my first speechless moment as a chaplain. I made a mental note to never again speak those words to anyone. Over the years, however, I have come full circle in my thinking, believing the words of my ministerial youth. *I like to believe somewhere in the recesses of an unconscious mind God is still able to reach us.* "Our God is in the Heavens; he does all that he pleases" (Psalm 115:3 ESV).

Calm

Returning to my office, I bow my head and weep for lost lives, for dreams wrecked by disease, for the loneliness of those left behind. I weep for the pain of separation and for the pain of togetherness. I weep for what the years can do, and for those who will never have them. And I weep for an inability to restore what has been taken from so many. I thank God for a night which ends as it began, with an awareness of grace upon each one who enters here, including myself.

11

A Shift in the Universe

I am paged to the emergency department. The charge nurse explains a young patient is being transported to our facility by emergency medical technicians after being pulled from under a car. Barely a teen, he joined in a *game* with neighborhood friends which involved dodging traffic. He is in critical condition, and I am told his father is on his way to the hospital. The invincible self-perception youths often possess can prove resilient and courageous. And though we are unaware, on this day it will bring heartbreak and devastation.

I greet the boy's father in the waiting area. He is tall, young, possibly mid-thirties. I lead him to the ED family room. His demeanor is tense as he braces for the unknown. He asks if I know what is going on. Determining what the boy's father has been told, I ask about information he has received concerning his son's accident. He replies he knows only that his son was hit by a car. I assure him our medical team is astute with communication and he will be given specifics as soon as they are able to determine them. And I wait with him. I am aware the emotional and mental well-being of this young father is at the forefront of the minds and hearts of all attending staff, second only to his son . . .

In those moments of waiting—when lives have not been forever changed, hearts have not yet broken, and hope has not been lost—were it in my power, there would be no damming end, as we sit and talk quietly of who this child is. We talk ball teams and academic challenges and gifts. We discuss the spirit of this boy whom parents brought into the world loving him more than anyone on earth. If it were within my power, we would remain protected by the insulated walls of this waiting room. I would bring coffee and be here to witness the message of hope and healing from the physicians. I do not want to help make the calls that loved ones should come to share the shock and grief. Were it within my power, we would ward off knowing anything other than the attributes and anticipated future of the terrific kid with loving parents.

The ED administrative assistant arrives to gather logistical information from the father and informs him the physician will update him shortly. He looks at her and asks, "What do you know?"

She hesitates briefly before answering, "It's serious."

I ask the boy's father if he would like me to pray with him. He replies, "I'm not a religious man, but I want to pray for my son." We pray for this father's precious boy whose life is presently in expert hands. In that moment, I was painfully aware that his son could have died, even while we prayed for him.

As we await the physician update, I ask about the boy's mother and learn the father has full custody. Still, I gently suggest, "Should you speak with her?" He does not want to call her yet. His voice full of agony, he tells me he took the boy to give him a better life.

The physician enters the room, introduces himself, and sits directly across from the boy's father. I have been in this room before, with other physicians, with other families. Although I do not want to, I recognize the facial expression, the body language of this kind physician focused upon his young patient's father. He leans in close, and speaks in a low, clear tone, "You son's condition is serious. His pelvis is fractured, and he has brain damage. How much, we do not know, but I believe it is extensive." The father looks the physician deeply in the eyes, as with the hope he has missed something better than what he has just heard. The physician informs the father he is sending his son to a pediatric hospital nearby for pediatric neurologists to examine him. Everything the father does after this appears to be rote. He has lost his light, and this night he will lose his son.

There are no words which can console a parent immediately following the loss of a child. There is no touch, no prayer, nothing, which can bring a mother or father back from those terrible moments. Only time, interwoven with the willingness to accept God's strength, can touch unfathomable grief to bring light out of the darkness. Only God. When a child is born, parents fall more and more deeply in love as the child grows. Following the unspeakable loss of a child, Heaven is the only place where parents reunite with that child to find continuance of their love throughout eternity.

The Physician's Eyes

At times, physicians, unfortunately, have the daunting task of communicating bad news. A physician I worked with for many years once paged me during a particularly difficult case, "Can you come to the ICU and talk with this family? You know I don't do emotions." The truth is, if he did not *do emotions*, he would not have sent for me. But I kept his secret.

The New York Times article, "Facing End-of-Life Talks, Doctors Choose to Wait" (2010) polled four thousand physicians overseeing cancer treatments. When asked when they discussed poor prognosis and end-of-life issues, 65 percent said they would initiate discussions relating to prognoses, though only 44 percent were likely to include end-of-life issues. The article states some physicians believe discussing poor prognoses in addition to end-of-life issues may cause patients to lose hope; however, the study further showed some initial difficult questions tabled indefinitely because of physician discomfort in discussing end-of-life issues.

Delivering bad news is never easy. Although hope is important, patients who ask the tough questions are usually braced to hear and begin processing answers. Even so, mental and emotional stressors remain for the physician who must deliver information which can conceivably rob a patient and family of normalcy, and physicians often understandably struggle during this shared journey. As the inspiration to *become* a physician is often based on a desire to heal, "First do no Harm" does not always feel congruent with delivering devastating news. Even so, physician and patient will etch out a path to continue, or to face the unimaginable together.

12

"Pray for Me"

In a hospital chapel sits a crystal bowl, and beside it, a note paper and pen. Ambulatory patients, families, and staff may leave prayer requests here. One of the most humbling things I will ever do as a chaplain is to offer up the prayers of others. Often gut-wrenching, these prayers touch the spiritual core of my being: "Let my grandpa get better; Help my husband through this surgery; Let my family get through Christmas without my sister; Help us to pay our rent this month; Help me find work; Give us the strength to take our mother off life support." And one, written in in a child's hand, I keep in my office to remind me of innocence: "Bring me a puppy." These prayers represent purity of faith in their petitions to the heart of God.

Standing in the gap gives me pause, for who am I to read the intimate requests of those in the throes of need? Only with deep humility may I become the intercessor for these heartfelt pleas of my fellowman, careful not to leave any prayer unattended or overlook praying any entrusted request.

I am a servant of God, a servant of the patient and family, and a servant of the hospital staff I am pledged to support. I accept the responsibility to pray for those who have written out their prayers in faith, and often in deep sorrow. In my human state, at times I am at a loss for adequate words to offer for those I do not know, for those who place such belief that the message of a little piece of paper will be delivered to Gods own ear. So, I lift the papers heavenward, at times without spoken word, as the Holy Spirit in my soul petitions God's mercy for those who ask, "Pray for me."

When Words Fail

Feeling overwhelmed with deep pain or emotion, one may find no words. Our distraught brokenness struggles with how to pray. In our great desire for God to hear, a desperate search ensues for the *right* words. The Creator of the universe knows our condition always. The Holy Spirit cries out to God without words: "The Spirit helps us in our weakness. We do not know what we ought to pray for, but the Spirit himself intercedes for us" (Romans 8:26 NIV). And silence, at times, prays the loudest. "Be still and know that I am God" (Psalm 46:10).

God offers assurance of his compassions, "As a father has compassion on his children, so the Lord has compassion . . ." (Psalm 103:13 CSB). God remembers we are vulnerable. He thinks about us, always. "How precious also are thy thoughts unto me, O God! How great is the sum of them! If I should count them, they are more in number than the sand" (Psalm 139:17, 18 KJV). He understands our pain; "The Lord is near to the brokenhearted . . ." (Psalm 34:18 NIV). The temple veil ripped from the top to the bottom as Christ took his last breath (Mark 15:37). The entire world turned black. God the Father, whose perfect Son was crucified, understands pain and injustice.

"The Lord will watch over your coming and going both now and forevermore" (Psalm 121:8 NIV). He is compassionately aware and watchful, "I will not forget you! See, I have written your names upon the palms of my hands" (Isaiah 49:15-6 NLT).

When we are unable to pray, God understands every word we cannot say. He is familiar with us, every detail, and he is merciful; ". . .Thou hast considered my trouble. Thou hast known my soul in adversities" (Psalm 31:7 KJV). The difficulties in finding the right words to pray at times may be our perfect communication.

Patient Quotes

"Good people are never in the way." (To the nurse who apologized for interrupting our conversation.)

"God has taught me it is just easier to do the right thing."

"Transform your fears into faith and you will inherit the freedom of the earth!"

"May God watch between you and me until we meet again."

"I'm not in denial. I know what is happening to my body. I just choose to focus on living."

"You will either be a light in the darkness, or you will be pulled into the darkness."

13

Chaplain Support, Ltd.

My evening transitions quickly as I note a referral from the step-down unit and make my way to the patient's room. Nearing the end of a long shift, emotional fatigue threatens. I enter the room to a palpable heaviness. Difficult to identify this weighty apprehension, I am familiar with the heaviness of grief—the weight of worry or stress. This is different; this is the heaviness of evil, and it unlocks my entire alert system.

The patient is propped up against the white hospital pillow which accentuates his dark hair and pallor. He smiles, introducing his wife who is sitting in a chair on the far side of the bed. She stands and takes a step nearer her husband. Her striking red hair is brushed back and falls over her shoulders. I look into the patient's face, eyes appearing as black liquid, cornea almost indistinguishable from pupil—mesmerizing. The atmosphere possesses an odd intensity as I take in a breath.

I ask, "What can I do for you?"

The patient replies, "I am a high priest of Wicca." When I do not immediately respond, he continues, "Do you know what that is? Wicca?"

"Wiccan?" I respond.

From behind me now, his wife laughs. "He is kidding," she states. My gaze returns to the patient, and I see he is not.

I inquire, "You asked for me?"

"Because I wanted to find out why you do this," he answers, spreading his hands out as he speaks. He eyes shimmer, his expression is taunting, subtlety defiant. Something indignant stirs inside me.

"I'm sorry," I tell him, matching his gaze. "I'm not sure why you asked for me. Are there spiritual needs either of you have?" No reply. He only smiles. His wife looks at him, again issuing a low amused laugh. I say goodnight and leave the room.

I check in with the nurse and leave the unit. Returning to my office, I reflect upon my studies under an astute Clinical Pastoral Education supervisor six years earlier. A former Catholic Priest, this brilliant mentor used his experience and communication skills to teach of unexpected challenges. A shortage of tact was part of his charm. He shared with his students his difficult decision to separate from the priesthood and marry the woman he loved. He taught strength and discernment, as well as direction when refusing others to misuse our presence, and spiritual boundary setting as a necessary decision for the mental, emotional, and spiritual health of all involved.

14

The Miracle of Death

I sit beside my last patient of this day. His eyes are closed, and I wonder what he has seen. His arms at his side, I think of the loved ones he has embraced. I consider the thousands of miles his feet, now motionless, have traveled during his journey. He has now come to this place. With me. The night is calm and quiet. Prayers have been prayed. Family has gone. And on this holy ground, I witness the miracle of death.

I have come to realize, as in birth, death is a miracle as well. Medically termed, "the dying process," the body wears out or is broken beyond repair, and the spirit readies itself to leave. The body, as it becomes uninhabitable, assists the spirit. A remarkable body knitted together in perfection through holy creativity is designed with fingers to grasp and touch, eyes to behold, ears to hear the symphony of the world, an interacting voice, and chords enabled to sing an entire scale of notes. Legs adjust to speed and tough feet withstand terrain—all incredible parts of the whole. Inside the head, a masterful operating element is surrounded by a protective skull. The chest contains a perpetual modem, which *feels,* and sometimes breaks even though surrounded by a cage of bones. Blood, circulating and warm, carries life-sustaining elements throughout. "I will praise You; for I am fearfully and wonderfully made. Marvelous are Your works, and that my soul knows very well" (Psalm 139:14 NKJV). Wonderfully made, purposefully unable to continue without the spirit.

When the spirit leaves, the body changes immediately, becoming void of that which gave it definition, character, and personality. The strong life force no longer permeates the body. Miraculously, the *person* has gone. The spirit has another destination.

"Now He who has prepared us for this very thing is God, who has given us the spirit for a guarantee. Therefore, we are always confident, knowing while we are at home in the body, we are absent from the Lord. For we walk by faith and not by sight. We are confident, yes, well pleased, to be absent from the body and present with the Lord" (2 Cor. 5:6-8).

Hey Papa and Granny, What Are You Doing Today?

My maternal grandparents died within a year of one another—not unusual when couples have spent a lifetime together. Shortly after my grandmother's passing, my grandfather followed her to Heaven. Their strong love and my grandmother's spiritual influence led me to petition God to see her or experience her spirit following their deaths. I prayed to see her in a vision or dream, especially during stressful times. In my role as a chaplain, patients and families shared accounts of seeing or sensing loved ones after their passing. In addition, my mother shared her own account of sensing *her* grandmother's presence more than once. I read of other accounts, and because my grandmother had been our family's spiritual matriarch, it seemed logical she would come to comfort me, and to perhaps say goodbye once more.

During my initial grief, I never saw or sensed either grandparent, and came to trust if God deemed I should, he would allow it. In future years, I did hear my grandmother's voice in dreams, and at times sensed my grandfather or grandmother near me in spirit. I came to believe we never needed another farewell because "goodbye" is not always necessary when you understand there will be a future. As I came to gain more understanding about Heaven through patients who were facing death, I formed a strong belief that my grandparents continued to watch over and act as intercessors for our family.

I believe something as loving, intelligent, and powerful as the human spirit does not simply forget about those who remain behind when making an earthly departure. I believe the awareness of family continues as loved ones converse with God on our behalf, as does Christ Jesus. I have "talked" to both my grandparents at times; "Hi, what are you doing up there today, Papa and Granny? Are you sewing angel wings, Granny? Are you tending to a Heavenly garden, Papa, with perfect giant green beans and squash?"

It is a beautiful winter's day as I drive to the hospital. I tell my grandmother I deeply desire to see her. I tell God I *need* to see her. I am *heavy* with the illness and death of the hospital. I reflect upon the Biblical account of Heaven's beauty and glory, so often shared with my patients: "Eye hath not seen, nor ear heard, neither have entered into the heart of man, the things which God hath prepared for them that love him" (1st Cor. 2:9 KJV).

As I drive over the Chesapeake Bay, with its outreach of beautiful waters, God grants my vision. I see my grandmother high up upon a mountain, standing on the edge of a cliff. Her arms are lifted out slightly behind her, her light robe blowing out softly. Her face is full of wisdom and beauty. I see my grandmother is a strong woman in the Heavens, and that her fears are gone. No storms, no cancer. I feel the presence of other strong women who will join her, leading in Heavenly places—my mother, as well as my loyal confidant and best friend who journeyed to Heaven before me. God places in my heart the knowledge that I will take my place among them one day, as will my daughters. All past and future sisterhoods of believing women, standing in their places on the mountain tops. And I understand, this is all I need to know for now.

15

Stoic

I check referrals and prioritize a *comfort care* request by family for chaplain support, indicating the patient could be nearing death. At this juncture, the patient or family may have chosen a less aggressive treatment plan other than medications to keep the patient comfortable. To effectively offer spiritual support near end-of-life, sensitivity to verbal and non-verbal cues is essential, as the needs of each patient and family differs.

I enter and introduce myself, witnessing various facial expressions and degrees of discomfort, perhaps even bewilderment, concerning participation in what is not a normal family gathering. Members introduce themselves, and as we chat, I sense a general anxiety concerning their anticipated loss. Grief already takes center stage. Family dynamics, though not appearing especially cohesive, reflect a stoic posturing—an attempt to remain in control. I get that.

Often in larger families, there is a spokesperson, whether self-appointed or family designated, who also acts to keep family members grounded. No obvious core person speaks for this family, though each member exhibits a calm though slightly nervous awareness of the situation. Each person quietly speaks, and I am moved by their vulnerability—poised, dignified, purposefully so. Their expressions tell of deeper thoughts and feelings, and my heart longs to help them normalize what is unspoken. I want to say, "There is no wrong or right way to do this, lose someone you love," though in this moment, these seem not the right words.

Several family members are seated on the elongated window seat which doubles as a cot in the hospital room. They have positioned themselves so they are not touching. At times, the very act of being close summons deep emotions. For those holding on to control, this may elicit an avoidance of proximity. I sense this family working hard to remain strong, and as we continue to interact, facial expressions appear akin to relief. Though they do not physically reach out to comfort one another or the patient. I consider I have entered during a family's concentrated effort to hold onto what they are comfortable with, their familiar dignity. They share a knowledge of what they must face as death unwittingly summons a valiant desire to cope, and to cope *well*. Enters one chaplain, whom they hope will make it easier.

During our conversation, three adult daughters make introductions, and their only brother as well. I look at the patient to see he has opened his eyes. I acknowledge him by name, as he gives a weak smile. Well groomed, the patient is wearing pajamas rather than a hospital gown, and the sheet is folded across his chest. He pulls it up higher with slender hands bearing well-kept nails, and his snow-white hair is neatly combed. I ask, "Are you warm enough?"

In a low tone, the patient answers, "I am, thank you. How are you?"

"I'm good, sir, thank you. I see you have a lot of love around you." I believe this to be true.

At times when a loved one nears death, family members experience uncertainty in expressing their feelings. Each one faces the task of handling his or her own emotions and, ironically, expressions of love may open feelings of pain, grief, or even guilt—those things held beneath the surface. Loved ones sometimes attempt to protect the patient emotionally by avoiding intensified emotions themselves. Family members usually understand and respect one another's need for strength in coping. It can be difficult for loved ones to be expressive, yet strong enough to say goodbye.

"I believe I do." He smiles and nods off slightly. If this gentleman wishes to pray, I want to meet his need, yet avoid interrupting his rest.

"I understand you have a Christian denominational background. Would you like me to pray with you?" His adult children look at him and wait for his answer.

"I would," he says quietly.

I look toward the four siblings, "Join us if you would like." The family comes to the bedside and each folds his or her hands in front. I step back around one of the daughters so she can stand near her father. The patient's son stands on the other side at the head as the two remaining daughters stand near the foot. The patient's children neither reach to take his hand nor the hand of a sibling. Out of respect for their comfort, I do not reach for their hands, or suggest we join hands as I often would. I do, however, reach out and place my hand over the patient's. After the prayer, the son places his hand on his father's shoulder. They all remain standing at the bedside.

"Dad, we love you," says the patient's son. The others nod in agreement or softly verbalize the same. His father looks up at his adult children and nods.

"I know you do." He says, "I love you too." He looks at his son a moment longer. "I'm proud of all you've done," he says, then closes his eyes. His son, tears welling up, sits back down. His sisters are wiping their eyes. An intimate sharing has occurred, and I soon say goodbye, allowing them privacy. In this family, I sense a hesitation to express pain, and I do not want to thwart an opportunity they may have to support one another. In a different situation with another family, perhaps I would remain longer. Handing them my card, I ask, "Is there anything else I can do?" The family agrees there is not, and each one stands to offer a handshake and word of appreciation. I tell them and their father it has been my honor and blessing to meet them, and it has. I thank them for allowing me to spend this time with them.

Though I bring spiritual support, I am still a stranger amid those in pain. Families sometimes need togetherness, and a part of supporting them is recognizing the timing and importance of this. Sensitivity involves helping a family engage enough to acknowledge the strength and presence of one another.

I cannot eliminate death, but I can briefly accompany those who journey through this loss. I cannot make it easier, but I can minister to the spiritual needs of those in pain. Returning to my office, I weep as I reflect upon the patient's strong resemblance to my German grandfather who died at ninety-two. Ministry to my patient has reminded me of his gentleness and strength.

The Patient

In another, I saw my grandfather today,
    Though he looked so frail and weak.
White as snow, his hair was combed,
    So caringly and neat.
And when he saw me in his room,
    It came as no surprise,
He gazed at me and held a smile
    With German sky-blue eyes.
My heart remembered stories true
    Of great times in his life.
Of courage and of honor,
    And one true love, his wife.
I bent down low beside his bed,
    And whispered in his ear,
"I'll pray with you,"
    At ninety-two, he'd nothing left to fear.
And as his gaze turned upward,
    There awaited Heaven's door,
Opened wide and welcoming,
    As I held his hand once more.
He closed his eyes in peace and slept

As I turned to walk away,
When in a face I had never met,
I saw my grandfather today.

Jan Moberg

We are all connected at times . . .

16

Meet People Where They Are

Advice and encouragement offered to anyone caring for a loved one with a critical illness or nearing end-of-life involves listening closely to the recipient of their care. During such a vulnerable time, the patient may view his or her caregiver or loved one as a place for life review. A critically ill individual often looks back over his or her life, sharing privileged thoughts previously unverbalized. Emotions of grief, anger, and regret may surface. Thoughts and feelings regarding family dynamics, alienations, confessions of past sins, and at times, resignation, may be voiced, as well as hope. But the main thing is to hear. This perspective will come home to me in a few short years as we care for my mother. My husband, a bonified type A, will be the *Mary* who listens, while I, *Martha,* will be less able to hear . . .

As the individual being cared for develops trust in his or her loved one or caregiver, private thoughts and life-review surfaces naturally, depending upon the medical condition of the patient. Though caregivers may be unable to resolve issues or grief, regret, or emotional pain, opportunities the patient finds to simply share may offer comfort and peace. My first chaplaincy supervisor once advised, "God was in the room before you came, and he will be in the room when you leave, so your continual goal is to allow God to work through you while you are there." Amazingly, this can happen without saying a lot, rather through intentional listening with empathy and compassion.

Upon entering ministry, I received invaluable advice from the wife of a colleague. "Always meet people where they are," she said. I cannot meet anyone where they are if I do not listen to their story. I cannot support the ill, the exhausted, overly stressed, worried patient or family if I cannot lay aside my own thoughts for a time and simply listen. Often, this is all anyone needs.

The Stars

"Lift your eyes and look to the Heavens: Who created all these; He who brings out the starry hosts one by one and calls them each by name. Because of His great power and might" (Isaiah 40:26 NIV).

God understands where we are in the scheme of things. In our solstices, He is aware of where we stand in relationship to others. At times, only God knows our hearts—the pain of separation when we are unsure of making things better or worse. We may place our loved ones, our own hearts, in God's mighty hands. Our *presence* is important to one another, and our presence is important to God. He created our being. He knows *our names*.

As a chaplain, I enter with what I know, which at times is *only a name*. Conversing with the patient, I gather information to discover patients as diverse as the stars. As additional information is shared among hospital staff, all disciplines crucial to the wellbeing of our patient become more familiar with each one. Also crucial to the patient's wellbeing is the love shared by family and friends, as medicinal as any treatment our team may render. For God to know us, to be present with us, He does not have to gather facts. He created the facts. He knows each patient, each of us, each heart and circumstance of our lives in detail. He understands . . .

"He determines the number of the stars and calls them each by name. Great is our Lord and mighty in power; his understanding has no limit" (Psalm 147:4-5 NIV).

The Medicinal Smile . . .

My colleague is paged to the emergency department to give emotional support to a stressed elderly gentleman. "Why are you upset, sir?" My colleague asks.

"The nurse has tried to castrate me three times!" The man angrily replies. "It's not going to work, and if she tries it again, I'm leaving!"

My colleague, temporarily speechless, stares at the much older man. Then it occurs to him, "Sir, do you mean 'catheterize?' The nurse tried to catheterize you?"

"That's right," The man answers. "And I'm leaving if she tries it again!"

Relieved, my colleague is barely able to suppress a smile as he gives this gentleman support to calm him, so the nurse can do her job as well.

Deathbed Confessions & Near-Death Experiences

Society has termed the phrase "deathbed confessions" to indicate those things a person wishes to get off his or her conscience near death, or to define an end of life turning to Christ. Judgement is unfortunately leveled at times, citing the individual's desire to rectify life only at the end. To this mindset, I offer, any confession or remorse for mistakes near death, whether for specific transgressions or in *coming to Christ,* is just as significant as at any other time. The unfortunate part for the individual is having missed knowing the greatness and love of God for a longer time on this side of Heaven, along with the fulfillment a relationship with Christ produces. Whether one has known and loved the Lord a lifetime or a moment, the grace which results overall is a heavenward eternity.

As believers brought to the mercy seat of Christ, growth is experienced in incremental moments throughout our lifetimes, strengthening our faith. What reveals the love of God to *you* may not convince *me,* though as we derive meaning from our diverse experiences, painful or joyous, they will guide us. I believe God appears before us in many ways, presenting opportunities to grow closer to Him. Free will enables us to say *no,* and for some, it takes illness or dying to say *yes.* No matter the lifestyle, the mistakes or poor decisions, deathbed confessions are accepted by our Lord and Savior, Jesus Christ. God is *always* willing to meet us where we are, as the forces of man's nature can never overcome the forces of God's grace.

17

Forgiveness is a Powerful Gift

Most of us have made wrong decisions, perhaps many. God knew we would be careless, even sinful. Scripture tells us we *will* at times fail to do the right thing. "For everyone has sinned; we all fall short of God's standard" (Romans 3:23 NLT). But God encourages us not to quit, not to give up. Paul puts it, "We can rejoice, too, when we run into problems and trials, for we know that they help us develop endurance. And endurance develops strength of character, and character strengthens our confident hope . . ." (Romans 5:3, 4). Paul's encouragement indicates we might find ourselves with stronger character following hard times, mistakes, challenges, and the changes we must sometimes make. "All discipline for the moment seems not to be joyful, but sorrowful; yet to those who have been trained by it, afterwards it yields the peaceful fruit of righteousness" (Hebrews 12:11 NASB).

Retrospection reveals those things learned the hard way may yield life's greatest lessons. Accepting God's forgiveness for our sins and mistakes is tantamount to a greater maturity in our Christian walk, yet at times it is difficult to embrace forgiveness and to accept self-forgiveness as well. Accepting God's forgiveness can bring greater freedom in stepping closer to our optimal being, helping us become more merciful toward others as well as ourselves.

> "Now one of the Pharisees was requesting Him to dine with him, and He entered the Pharisee's house and reclined at the table. And there was a woman in the city who was a sinner; and when she learned that He was reclining at the table in the Pharisee's house, she brought an alabaster vial of perfume, and standing behind Him at His feet, weeping, she began to wet His feet with her tears, and kept wiping them with the hair of her head, and kissing His feet and anointing them with the perfume. Now when the Pharisee who had invited Him saw this, he thought to himself, 'If this man were a prophet He would know who and what sort of person this woman is who is touching Him; that she is a sinner.'
>
> And Jesus answered him, 'Simon, I have something to say to you.'
> And he replied, 'Say it, Teacher.'
> 'A moneylender had two debtors: one owed five hundred denarii, and the other fifty. When they were unable to repay, he graciously forgave them both. So, which of them will love him more?'
> Simon answered and said, 'I suppose the one whom he forgave more.'
> And He said to him, 'You have judged correctly'" (John 7:36-43 NASB).

Refusing to accept God's forgiveness is counterproductive to the life God has for each of us. Holding to feelings and thoughts of unworthiness thwarts self-confidence and the ability to accomplish our goals and make the most of those opportunities and possibilities God presents. "Who hath saved us and called us with a holy calling, not according to our works, but in accordance with His own purpose and grace, which was given to us in Christ Jesus before the world began . . ." (2 Timothy 1:9 KJV).

Refusing to accept God's forgiveness is declaring Christ's suffering and death on the cross was not sacrifice enough to cover our sins—that the death of God's perfect Son in our place was not sufficient. Believing God's promises, because we are forgiven, strengthened, and led, not according to our transgressions, but according to His mercy and loving kindnesses.

Which of us will love him more?

Love and Purpose

Giving love is an essential involvement in the ministry of care. Paul says if we do not have love, we are simply making noise. Patients and loved ones in our charge are reminders of the importance of love and charity. Many moments affirm the choice to love and the choice of vocation. The fast-paced, ever-changing world of healthcare is filled with ongoing and complex challenges. Perhaps the most important reason for being in any role is to share love and caring. Each individual uniquely offers gifts of his or her personal style of love and care. "God has appointed these . . . apostles, prophets, teachers, miracles, gifts of healing, helps, administrations . . ." (1 Corinthians 12:28 NKJV). God has given each individual gifts, strengths, and purpose.

We hold to the faith God places accessible strength within us. Faith will not make us perfect, but it will allow us to be human. Relying upon this inner calm, even within our storms, we reach our greatest potential and purpose. There are times we feel inadequate, other times we feel accomplished, though in all circumstances, our daily help and renewal is in the strength of God who rests in us.

"There are different kinds of service, but the same Lord. There are different kinds of working, but in all of them and in everyone, it is the same God at work. Now to each one the manifestation of the Spirit is given for the common good" (1 Corinthians 12:5-7 NIV). Part of a great whole, we are all critical to the administration of caregiving and encouragement of one another. Together, we make a better whole, have better relationships—a better world.

18

"First . . . Believe as One of These"

"**I** have the results from my scan," Mom tells me. "There is a small mass in my subclavian artery; they think it could be cancer." I hold the phone very still.

"How sure are they?" I ask.

"Sure enough . . ." Mom replies.

"Ok, Mom," I tell her. "We will beat this again."

She is scared; we all are. Her oncologist schedules another scan, a closer look.

I am putting on make-up, getting ready for work, when my eleven-year-old son comes into my bedroom. "Hey, honey."

"Hi mom, morning," he says.

"Are you ready for school?" I ask.

"I'm ready," he says. He stands near my door looking rather pensive.

"Are you okay?" I ask.

"I'm good . . . Really good. Mom?" He asks.

"Yes, honey?"

"God told me, 'Don't worry about your grandmother.'" My son has my undivided attention. We are both silent. "Anyway, God told me that."

"Okay, honey. When did he tell you that?"

"I was praying for her last night. God told me not to worry about her anymore."

Inside I am in awe that God is talking to my son, and my son is listening. Why am I surprised? When my son was born, I, like Hannah, knew he belonged to God. Now he is delivering messages.

Three weeks later, Mother has her follow-up CT scan. The mass is gone; the CT scan shows the artery is clear.

"From the lips of children . . . You Lord have called forth Your praise (Matthew 21:16 NIV).

Young Boy, Old Soul

The spiritual or psychological needs for a child are no less important than those of any adult—perhaps simpler, more tender, trusting. A new consult in pediatrics formulates a mental picture of distraught parents in need of support. Though when I arrive on the unit, a smiling nurse greets me to say her eight-year-old patient has asked to see a chaplain. When I enter the room, the patient's mother and younger brother are at his side. I introduce myself and tell the young boy I understand he asked to see me. "Yes, I did," he replies. His mother asks if he would like time alone to talk with me, and the boy acknowledges he would.

After his mother and brother have left, I ask, "What would you like to talk about?"

"Sometimes I have a hard time breathing," the boy begins. "Then my heart starts to beat faster." We discuss his medical condition as well as the resulting complications. He knows them well.

I ask, "What do you do when you feel these changes in your body?" He tells me he runs to find one of his parents. "What do the changes make you think about?"

With experience beyond his eight years, this precious wide-eyed boy says, "I get scared. The doctor says my medicine is not working the way it should. He is trying to find a medicine that will work better. But now, we just end up in the hospital."

Wow, I think. I ask, "Do you talk about being afraid with your parents?"

"No, I don't want them to be scared too," the child replies. *Unbelievable*, I think.

"Do you think that would be a normal way for them to feel?" I ask.

"Yes, but if they think I'm scared, they will be *more* scared," he replies.

"Do you think they might be thinking the same thing?" I ask, and smile to reassure him the things we are discussing are good.

"Maybe," He says.

"You could ask them to talk about it," I suggest. "Sometimes understanding how someone else feels helps us to accept our own feelings and to help one another better. What do you think?"

Thoughtfully, he replies, "I think so. I want to."

I ask, "What do you think will happen when you talk with your parents?"

"I think it will be better. Maybe we can let my little brother listen. I'll ask my mom."

"And we can pray about these things?"

He smiles a boyish smile and tells me, "That's why I asked you to come!" I take his little hand and am reminded of the innocence of childhood and the tenderness of God. "Let the little children come to me . . . For the kingdom of Heaven belongs to such as these" (Matthew 19:14 NIV).

19

The Hospital Inn

The hospital has just finished building an additional wing. The new addition is a step up from the older wings, and the patients and families seem to appreciate the pleasant modern design. Among other amenities are tastefully crafted bay windows with built-in seating underneath which double as a sleeping area for family members. The rooms are painted in pretty, soft colors, and equipment is built into the walls. The patient rooms are not unlike nice hotel rooms, which we hope will be positive and comforting to those who enter.

I go to look in on a patient who experienced a fall while out to dinner with her gal friends. While exiting the restaurant booth, she unfortunately missed a step-down. Her friends call an ambulance which rushes her to our ED, and following a brief exam and x-ray, she is whisked off to surgery for a fractured hip repair. When my patient's friends come to visit, they find her sleeping and leave a note for her which reads, "You had better do what they say. We will be back." A short time later, I enter my patient's hospital room to find her appearing anxious. I ask if she is in pain and she replies hesitantly, "It's my *head* I'm concerned about." She tells me her account of what occurred.

The patient woke, disoriented, her last fuzzy recollection being of someone administering a drug to her. She says the room was pleasant, and she thought she was in a nice hotel. Reading the hand-written note from her friends, left on a piece of torn-off paper, she then realized her jewelry was missing. So, she came to the only conclusion which made sense. *She had been kidnapped!* She tells me she asked herself, "Why would anyone kidnap a seventy-year-old woman?"

My patient smiles, and with a slight blush relates the tip-off came when she discovered her call-bell. She says she looked down at her hospital gown as a murky recollection of her fall began seeping back into her consciousness, along with discomfort in her hip. We share a laugh in addition to a prayer and agree upon the moral of the story. "If you wake up in the *Hospital Inn,* ask for a chaplain before paying ransom!"

20

The Power of Healing

"And all the people tried to touch him, because power was coming from him and healing them all" (Luke 6:19 NIV).

My colleague and I are making rounds in Intensive Care. A man in his forties occupies one of the rooms, and his wife stands beside his bed holding his hand. As we enter, we realize she is praying and wait quietly while she finishes. We introduce ourselves and her excitement is such that I almost look back over my shoulder to see if someone else has come in. "We've been waiting," she says. "I asked for a chaplain and now we have two. I want you to help me pray for healing for my husband."

Specific prayer requests for healing made by family members or patients are a unique consideration for chaplaincy. I typically honor the request, and do not want to limit God in my thinking. "For the Kingdom of God is not in word, but in power" (1 Cor. 4:20 KJV). This is God's power, not mine. When a prayer for healing is requested, even for a patient likely to pass, I want to be a servant, a conduit of Christ to channel healing to those whose faith has brought them to ask. For "healing" is not limited to living, neither is it limited to the patient, as the requestor may receive healing power and strength as well. My task is to speak believing, "Our God is in heaven; He does whatever He pleases (Psalm 115:3 NKJV).

The faith of the patient's wife permeates the air. My colleague and I embrace the amazing grace present here. Each of us pray, as a wife embraces her husband in love and spirit. There is an element in prayer for healing—a necessity to let go as completely as possible, trusting in the power of an omnipotent God. There are no perfect words, nothing we have accomplished which entitles us to such a request. "To me, who am less than the least of all the saints, this grace was given" (Ephesians 3:8 NKJV).

As we offer these prayers, there is an alliance in our souls as the Holy Spirit unites us in agreement, one with the other. It is then quiet, peaceful. The patient, barely conscious, smiles at his wife, whose tears streak her face. In the following days, he improves enough to transfer from ICU, continuing to recover more quickly than his physicians anticipated, enough to go home. The medical staff calls it, "extraordinary." His wife calls it, "a miracle."

"Now to Him who is able to do exceedingly abundantly above all ye ask or think, according to the power that works in us, to Him be the glory" (Ephesians 3:20).

21

Being Present

I t is said a person may not always remember your presence, but they will not forget your absence. I have learned during serious illness or end of life, that which we most lament are lost connections. I have never heard an ill or dying patient spend an inordinate amount of time pining over inanimate objects. What we seem to desire most at these critical moments is the comfort of others—knowing those we love are present, at least in heart if not proximity. Although we want this *any time*, the difference is normally, we *have time*. In our minds, we can conceive a possible resolve to broken or damaged relationships which could happen at any moment, *except* when we are out of time.

Being present is normally easier when there is no chasm to jump. Scripture wisely advises, if possible, mend fences in the present. "As much as is possible, as much as it depends on you, live peaceably with all men (Romans 12:18 NKJV). This may seem a tall order, perhaps not always feasible. Humans are complex. We want peace, but when we have an opportunity to make it, often the words will not come, or our hearts are cold. In the safe spaces of our minds, we create possible scenarios of resolve, only to become emotionally or mentally overwhelmed when we face the situation in real time. Paul's advice in Romans helps us embrace reality. *As much as is possible, as much as it depends on you . . .* We must do the best we can. I have heard gut-wrenching cries from loved ones in shock who did not anticipate the critical illness or death of a loved one. We think there will be an opportunity to say, "I'm sorry." To say, "I love you." Sometimes that opportunity is taken.

Paul's message continues, "If someone has done you wrong, do not repay him with a wrong. Try to do what everyone considers to be good" (Romans 12:17 GNT). It is alright to reach out, even though you have been wronged, even if *you* have wronged someone. We each have the choice to reach out, and we each have the choice to reach back. *Try to do . . . good.*

I have learned not to assume *anything* regarding the end of life. I do not assume the patient cannot sense the presence of others. I do not assume he or she cannot hear. More than once, I have seen tears slide down the face of a patient neither alert nor oriented upon hearing a loved one's voice, or when a prayer was spoken. Sometimes dying individuals appear to sense things others cannot. In chaplaincy, I learned not to assume, only to journey beside—to be present.

Regret and Grace

"I wish I had . . . I wish I hadn't . . ."

An intense exploration for patients, and often families, is regret. Even the most caring individual will at times reflect upon words which could have been said, though left unspoken, or words said in haste or anger and left unapologetically. As a chaplain, I celebrate the fact that there is usually room for grace in most religions, and it is my privilege to guide the patient or family in embracing this. Whenever we give ourselves permission to be human, we remove heavy burdens from our psyche and our souls. We may then focus more completely upon the things at hand—the illness, injury, healing, loss, and at times, dying.

Patients who are hospitalized become still enough long enough to think about specific things. Relationships frequently top the list, including one's relationship with God. *I wish I had,* or *I wish I hadn't,* are among the most common statements I hear. I count it my privilege to listen, support, and respond when appropriate to these soulful introspections. In this way, "better" can be felt in the soul as well as the body. And "better" is vital when a seriously ill patient is living one day or even one hour at a time.

Relationships with family and loved ones are often prioritized in the mind and heart of an individual who is ill or approaching the end of life. Most of us do not plan to get sick, including those who may be estranged from family or loved ones. The person who enters the hospital is accompanied by the journey he or she has traveled. Therefore, becoming *still* facilitates becoming *thoughtful* regarding one's past. This seems to be a natural turn of events, as illness and hospitalization may precipitate restoration of relationships, whether literally or simply in the heart and mind. It is bittersweet to carry a message to one who did not anticipate losing or hearing from a critically ill mother, father, sister, brother, daughter, son . . . "He wanted you to know he loved you."

22

Love in the ICU

A patient in his sixties has taken an unexpected turn for the worse. Physicians have conferenced with his family, telling them he will pass, and possibly soon. The grief-stricken members surround his bed, including his beautiful wife. Barely conscious, he hears as his adult children express their love, his son fighting to remain strong, and his two daughters holding onto one another.

The patient's wife unabashedly climbs onto his ICU bed, running her pretty manicured fingers over his forehead and down his cheek. "I love you," she says, tears streaming down her face. "I love you and I don't know how to live without you. You taught me everything about love, about security, about sex. You taught me how to live, but you never taught me how to live without you. I don't know how to do that." I, the children, the nurses—we are all weeping profusely at this beautiful, raw display of grief and pure love. The children surround their parents, lying together on this ICU bed as we pray. It is difficult to follow love like that. Only God, in the Heavens, can. "Set me as a seal upon your heart, As a seal upon your arm; For love *is as* strong as death" (Song of Solomon 8:6 NKJV).

Through Unseen Grief

I stand quietly at the door of the patient's room. Her husband, an elderly black gentleman, is seated at her bedside. He rests his hands, one on the other, on the top of his wooden cane. He looks up as I enter, and I offer my hand as I introduce myself. I sit in a chair close to him and he begins to tell me of his loved ones, of those who care for him and his wife. He shares that he is not alone; there are family members and friends who support and watch over them. He slowly brings me into his inner sanctum of grief for the woman who, for many years, has been his comrade. She is now his quiet companion, gone into the recesses of a mind taken by the mysteries of aging. He misses her.

The man reaches out, touches her arm, and speaks her name. She raises her head off the pillow without opening her eyes, then rests it down once more. Her husband gently pinches her arm and repeats her name, a little louder this time. "Sometimes she knows I'm here," he looks at me with sadness. He says he is getting by, though I hear and see his unspoken message. He is heartbroken. He is lost without her. I extend my hand and we pray.

As he expresses his appreciation for our time together, I find it difficult to leave. God has placed this couple in my path but for a moment. If only I could do more, if only I could make everything right for them. I leave wishing this gentleman could go back and recapture his bride and his youth. I leave believing I will see them again and we will talk of amazing things on the other side of Heaven.

> "I love thee with a passion put to use
> In my old griefs, and with my childhood's faith.
> I love thee with a love I seemed to lose

With my lost saints,—I love thee with the breath,
Smiles, tears, of all my life!—and, if God choose,
I shall but love thee better after death."

Elizabeth Barrett Browning

23

Chasms

The room of my next patient is closed, though a quiet knock brings his adult daughter to the door. Speaking in a whisper, she tells me her father is sleeping. I quietly ask how he is doing. She answers, "As well as can be expected." When I ask how she is doing, tears well up and she tells me, "Better than yesterday. We are both fine," she offers, "but thank you for asking." Her father begins to thrash about in his bed, speaking unintelligibly. She steps back, reaching toward the bed curtain near the door. With this protective gesture, she nods slightly and says, "Good evening." I hand her my card, knowing my support is not something she will accept this night. Her endurances are being tested, and in this moment, she is stronger without discussions. I leave with an image of this daughter, exhausted and loyal, returning to her father's bedside . . .

My next patient is seated in an armchair bedside her bed. She smiles a wide smile as I extend my hand to take hers, and she immediately asks, "Where is the hospital?" I am hopeful she can connect and ask her name. She knows her name yet rambles on, asking nonsensical questions. Over years of chaplaincy, I have discovered a spiritual mystery and ask if she would like to pray. She looks at me and says simply, "Yes." Amazingly, an individual can forget everything and everyone, yet remember how to pray. How is it that a patient deep in the throes of dementia can recite the Lord's prayer? The 23rd Psalm?

We bow our heads and hold hands as I offer a short prayer. Afterwards, she returns her gaze to me and says, "We all need that." I agree, and this sweet, white-haired lady returns to her senseless babble. I thank her for spending time with me and she asks if I have a sister.

Hopeful, I tell her, "No."

She asks, "Can you drive a car there?"

As the respiratory therapist enters, I say goodbye. The patient smiles that big smile again. I would imagine her as charming in past years, as in her own way she still is. I think about those who have known and cared for this woman throughout her lifetime, and pray love remains in her world.

My next patient referral is out of her room. I recall passing an elderly lady seated in the hallway eating cooked vegetables. Knowing the nurses often seat patients who need extra attention near their station, I check to find this is the patient I am looking for. I find the frail, silver-haired lady picking up corn with her long slender fingers and throwing her head back to drop the kernels into her mouth. Kneeling beside the patient, I am uncertain as to whether she will understand my presence. I introduce myself and wait.

The conversation which follows is completely lucid, as I consider why the patient is seated near the nurses' station. She shares some details of her medical condition. She tells me about her family; we pray. She expresses her appreciation for my visit, and we say goodbye. As I turn to exit the unit, I hear this little lady issue an amazingly loud, blood-curdling scream! The nurse looks at me and calmly states, "She likes to *scream*. She seems happier here with us and disturbs other patients less." I am glad we were able to visit and smile to myself that we were able to chat without *incident*. God was there before me, and He will be there as I leave.

24

Ministering Through Personal Experience

My father is hospitalized with a sudden, serious illness. Only twenty years my senior and in excellent health, it is a shock when he experiences a sudden loss of energy and is unable to walk. Alarmingly, this highly intelligent man cannot hold a conversation. A diagnosis of severe pneumonia without classic symptoms follows several days of testing to rule out stroke and encephalitis, among other possibilities. Along with my family, I learn sudden serious illness can cause AMS, *altered mental status.*

Six hundred miles away, I ask Dad's physician whether I should travel to his bedside. Following a brief silence, the physician replies, "Not yet . . ." Having made calls to families for physicians myself, I deeply appreciate his position in this moment. Valuing the physician's expertise in the specialty of pulmonary, more than this, I value his sensitivity. In my work, I have witnessed families holding on to hope beyond reason. When we are given a *window* during which physicians wait for my father to "turn the corner," I will not consider any other outcome *except* recuperation. No outcome other than "better."

Personal experience coupled with years in the hospital environment has taught me we often continue to hope in the face of stark facts which contradict what we are hoping for. Neither love, nor hope, are exact sciences. They co-exist powerfully to assist us in fighting to continue if we can.

When my children were young, I watched renowned pediatrician and author T. Berry Brazelton take an easy-going approach to child rearing. He assured anxious parents, including myself that a child will eat when he or she is hungry, let go of the pacifier when old enough to be embarrassed, and drop the bottle prior to grade school. He held the view that only in rare instances do these milestones go unresolved naturally. Dr. Brazelton's approach normalized my concerns as a parent and gave me confidence that milestones typically occur as they should. This wisdom applies to the beginning of life. In my role as a chaplain and a daughter I have learned similar lessons regarding the challenges of life, and death as well.

Patients and families, including myself, hold onto hope for as long as they need to, and when they must, they will let go. Those left behind will seldom deny death when they face it, though the hope one holds to during critical illness and end-of-life scenarios often serves as a vital strength and coping strategy. If this is construed as denial, then we must wisely concede, as denial is not always a bad thing.

The spiritual faith we hold on to, as well as faith in one another, plays out each day in family, work, church, community, and around the world. This may include medical support, family and friend support, psychological support, grief support, and many other modes of *strength-lending*. As simple as a phone conversation or as complex as being a prime caregiver, hope, faith, and support can involve a minute, or a lifetime. It is the care and compassion evidenced in the spirit of humankind.

Dad's physician notifies me, Dad is alert and oriented, though still slightly agitated, giving the nurses hell as he is not yet allowed to get up. Having no doubt Mom will keep him in check, our family is thankful and relieved as Dad recuperates fully, returning to his home in the mountains that he loves.

Somewhere in Time

My mother is sent to a coli-rectal specialist for an evaluation and is consequently scheduled for a colon resection. My father is told the surgery will take approximately five hours if there are no problems. Hours into surgery, Mother's blood pressure drops and the surgical team temporarily loses her vitals. She is resuscitated and the surgery is successfully finished. Days later, she shares:

> "Somewhere in time, I experienced the most miraculous moments of my life. Standing in the doorway of the surgical suite, I saw a beautiful man in a white robe. He stretched out his hand to me, and I tried desperately to reach him. Then, suddenly, I was back, the surgery team yelling my name. I learned later that I had been in surgery nine hours. I cannot say I was fully conscious, but on the second day after surgery, as the sun was shining through my hospital window, the church's music director and his wife were seated in front of the window and appeared as angels. Not a day passes that I do not recall this experience. I saw a glimpse of Heaven. I met Christ."

The event my mom experienced caused our family to ponder even more deeply those things awaiting us. Her near-death experience provided evidence we could never otherwise witness on earth, on this side of Heaven . . .

25

Prayer, Worry, & Anxiety

God often meets a need following a time of conscious petitions, our prayers. A period spent waiting for answers may contribute to spiritual growth, a better understanding of timing, or other forms of wisdom. Prayer, in addition to communication with God, is recognition of his love and provision, and answers come in many forms, including *no* or *not at this time*. It is humbling to recognize God's love in the form of the opening *or* closing of doors, as he knows our needs infinitely better than we ourselves. "And my God shall meet all your needs according to the riches of his glory in Christ Jesus" (Philippians 4:19 NIV).

At times, we come anxiously to God as though He is unaware of our concerns or has forgotten us. ". . . I will never forget you! See, I have written your name on the palms of my hands" (Isaiah 49:15-16 NLT). God communicates as a loving Father, "Be anxious for nothing, but in everything by prayer, let your requests be made known to God, and the peace of God which surpasses all understanding will guard your hearts and minds through Christ Jesus" (Philippians 4:6-8 NKJV). Holding to our faith through worrisome or anxiety-producing events or time-periods, we can be certain God is holding us. Reflecting upon these empowering verses, my prayer dialog may go something like this:

"Be anxious for nothing . . ." (Scripture)
"Really?" (Me)
"For nothing."
"For *nothing?*"
"Be anxious for nothing."

My grandmother once said she felt deep anxiety during an especially challenging time in my life. After praying for me throughout the day, she began to prepare dinner. As Granny reached down to the potato bin, she said in that precise moment, God lifted her. My grandmother recounted her feet left the kitchen floor. Familiar with Granny's strong faith, I never doubted this sacred event. She said this was an amazing moment in her Christian walk, and she did not feel anxious about me anymore. Smiling, she added, "That day!"

Vulnerable, even in faith, we swiftly reclaim our human frailties. Over again, we must recall the miracles and the mercies, to trust in God's word and purpose for our lives. Experiencing or hearing of momentous spiritual happenings, from scripture in historical biblical times or from a revered spiritual grandmother, we must remember the strength God makes available and the purposes he makes visible in your life and in mine.

Fear and Stress

Stress is the extra demand made on the body and mind during tense or difficult times. The automatic nervous system releases hormones into the blood stream, causing chemical changes as the heart beats faster, breathing speeds up, and blood surges to the brain. This causes one to fight the danger or attempt to flee.

There is also an enemy, *a peace-taker.* "Be vigilant because your adversary, the devil is walking about as a roaring lion, seeking whom he may destroy" (1 Peter 5:8). Satan celebrates defeat. He whispers words of judgment and despair, especially to those who are vulnerable during stressful or problematic times. Remember, *God is always stronger, no exceptions.* "Greater is he who is in you than he who is in this world" (1 John 4:4 KJV). When anxieties produce fear, accept God's comfort: "Fear not, for I am with you; be not dismayed, for I am your God. I will strengthen you, Yes, I will help you . . ." (Isaiah 41:10 NKJV). When fear develops into chronic worry, "I tell you not to worry about everyday life . . ." (Matthew 6:25 NLT).

The living word of God has been proven the most authentic historical book in existence, though we hesitate at times to believe it lives for us. My years of experience in living may add up to a millisecond in God's time, though at times I still forget to solicit strength from an omnipotent, omniscient, eternal God. I forget about my mustard seed and become fearful. "Fear not, for I am with you . . ." My own experience has taught me to take the hand of my fearful patients, saying, "Presently, you may not be filled with faith, but you have this much faith," taking my pen to make a tiny dot in the center of his or her palm, and I share, "Christ tells us it is enough."

Finding peace in times of stress requires awareness of personal limitations and strengths. Identifying *stress increasers*, such as feelings of insufficiency, insecurity, anger, disappointment, or guilt allows us to acknowledge these emotions to God, who bears our concerns while helping us overcome challenges. This works to develop character and purpose, realizing the strength and possibilities in surrendering burdens of the past, as well as present grievances. Giving Christ our burdens is freeing, as we work toward forgiving ourselves and others, making this a conscious effort in our relationship with Christ and those around us.

When my husband was a boy, their visiting minister carved the reference, "Proverbs 3:5-6," on the banister in his family's home. Guidance from that scripture has spoken to my husband throughout his lifetime, often coming back during times of stress. "Trust in the LORD with all your heart and lean not unto your own understanding; in all your ways acknowledge Him, and He shall direct your paths" (Proverbs 3:5-6 NKJV). Scripture tells us not to worry, be anxious, or afraid because God knew we would be. He compassionately guides us with sound instruction concerning our state of mind and spirit, comforting and lovingly directing us through fear or worry.

Embrace relationships which enable respectful openness and honesty. Having one close relationship where comfort exists in being oneself and sharing just about anything can rival the best therapy. Do what you love on a regular basis. Talk with God as a friend, a Father, and a King. He will provide you the strength and grace to cope with stress. "Though I walk in the midst of trouble, you will revive me . . ." (Ps. 138:7 NKJV).

As a child, I played in the woods behind my home. I knew just how far into the woods I could go without venturing into unfamiliar surroundings. One day, however, I was feeling adventuresome and walked further into the woods. After what seemed a short distance, I turned to head in what I thought was the direction of home, quickly realizing I was not returning to familiar surroundings. Initially unalarmed, I became more anxious as minutes passed. Changing course, still unable to find my way, I began running in one direction, then the other. Soon, in full-blown panic mode, I called, "Daddy! Daddy!" Eventually screaming into what seemed like empty air, the friendly forest became an ominous wood.

After a time, the most comforting sound I could imagine reached my ears—my dad answering, calling my name. "Jan, Jan! Can you hear me?" Following the sound of his voice, I called back, "I'm here!" My father's voice led me to the safety of familiar woods and the beautiful clearing surrounding our home. That clearing and my father's arms felt like Heaven. In the years since, I have learned, no matter how lost we become spiritually, emotionally, mentally, or literally, our Heavenly Father's voice will always lead us home. "But now, this is what the Lord says . . . 'Do not be afraid—I will save you—I have called you by name. You are mine. I will make a path through the wilderness . . .'" (Isaiah 43:1, 19 GNT).

Fatigue

Physical, mental, and emotional depletion at times require a conscious, active regrouping. When kids ask for money, parents sometimes say, "I'm all *tapped out.*" We can become tapped out in other areas as we meet responsibilities and attempt to cope with daily demands while caring for others. We may experience spiritual fatigue. There exists a remedy for our exhaustion and a path to spiritual renewal.

"He gives power to the weak, and to those who have no might He increases strength. Even the youths shall faint and be weary. And the young man shall utterly fall, but those who wait upon the Lord shall renew their strength; they shall mount up with wings like eagles, they shall run and not be weary, they shall walk and not faint" (Isaiah 41:29-31 KJV).

There is a way to meet challenges which, ironically, requires a decision to rest. "Come to me, all ye who labor and are heavy laden and I will give you rest. Take my yoke upon you and learn from me, for I am gentle and lowly in heart, and you will find rest for your souls" (Matthew 11:28). These words of Christ contain solid direction. Taking the *yoke* of Christ involves learning and *leaning.* A yoke is built to distribute the work of the oxen and relieve the burden of each. We are *yoked* to Christ when we allow Him to teach us skills of the plow, direction, and the sharing of our burdens. When our spirits are at rest, we find renewal in other areas resulting in more energy, less worry, and increased positivity.

The God who formed us in our mother's womb knows when we are weary, providing a way to rest and regroup. "For you created my inmost being; you knitted me together . . ." (Psalm 139:13 NIV). The God who knows the number of hairs on our heads knows the number of stressors in our lives. "And even the hairs of our head are all numbered" (Matthew 10:26).

When our concern is performance, we may avoid rest, assuming the scriptural character of Martha: "As Jesus and his disciples were on their way, he came to a village where a woman named Martha opened her home to him. She had a sister called Mary, who sat at the Lord's feet listening to what he said. But Martha was distracted by all the preparations that had to be made. She came to him and asked, 'Lord, don't you care that my sister has left me to do the work by myself? Tell her to help me!'

"'Martha, Martha' the Lord answered, 'you are worried and upset about many things, but few things are needed – or indeed only one. Mary has chosen what is better, and it will not be taken away from her'" (Luke 10:38-42 NIV). We need rest and restoration, as well as the discipline needed, at times, to rest.

God strengthens our bodies, minds, and souls. As we trust in God's strength through each concern, we become stronger as well. "He said to me, 'My grace is sufficient for you, for My power is made perfect in weakness,' therefore I will rather boast all the more gladly about my weaknesses, so that Christ's power may rest on me" (II Cor. 12:9 NIV). Truth for the apostle, Paul, remains true for us today.

It is an exciting part of our spirituality to realize when our inner strength wanes, that we can rest in Christ, operating under His power. When we take our weaknesses before the King, it is then we are strong. "Let us fix our eyes on Jesus, the author and finisher of our faith, who for the joy set before him endured the cross, scorning its shame, and sat down at the right hand of the throne of God. Consider him who endured such opposition from sinful men, so that you will not grow weary and lose heart" (Hebrews 12:2). The sacrifice of Christ is sufficient, enabling us to live forgiven and strengthened in the unique and positive destiny God has planned for each one of us—for you, and for me.

26

Faith, Questions, and Trials

The book of Job serves as an example of solace when we question circumstances, suffering, or God and is designed to give us hope and strengthen our faith during trials. The man, Job, is described in the beginning chapter as *blameless* and *upright*. Satan contends this is solely because God favors Job, and according to scripture, God allows him to be tested. In the space of a day, Job loses his children, flocks, and staff. Ripping his clothing and shaving his head in sorrow, he continues to worship God though he is afflicted with skin sores covering his body. Even Job's wife urges him to denounce God—to give up and die.

Three of Job's friends arrive, initially sitting in silence out of respect for his suffering. Soon Job and his friends begin to debate the *whys* of what has befallen him. The dialog reflects mankind's need to understand injustice, as Job's friends attempt to make sense of what has befallen a good and obedient man. They *surmise* as to why Job would experience ungodly travails and suggest to Job, though he has helped others, perhaps he failed to realize their pain. His friends also suggest Job may have forgotten sin lurking in his past. Lastly, they hypothesize Job's children may somehow be to blame for his dilemma. By chapter thirteen, Job has essentially had it with his well-meaning friends, calling them *worthless* and practically advising them to *shut up,* as he defends God's greatness. "You are worthless . . . If only you would be altogether silent! For you, that would be wisdom" (Job 13:4, 5 NIV).

By chapter thirty, Job questions his own suffering. He ponders deeply what he could have done to deserve such pain, pointing out in his defense those things he has done *right*. "Surely no one lays a hand on a broken man when he cries for help in his distress. Have I not wept for those in trouble? Has not my soul grieved for the poor? Yet when I hoped for good, evil came; when I looked for light, then came darkness" (30:24-26).

Though a man of strong faith, Job is *still* a man, as overwhelming circumstances present the temptation to give up. This choice serves as a mental safety mechanism for giving up; one surmises no further injury can be inflicted. Even in declaring defeat, however, there often remains a minute amount of hope. Job, confused and afraid, desires understanding; he dares to hold on to hope. "Should he be told I want to speak? . . . In his justice and great righteousness, he does not oppress . . . Does he not have regard for all the wise in heart?" (Job 37: 20, 23-24).

God speaks. "I will question you, and you shall answer me. Where were you when I laid the earth's foundations? Tell me if you understand. Who marked its dimensions? Surely you know" (Job 38:1,2). Though God questions Job's in turn, it is not without enlightenment as God eloquently describes his power. "Do you give the horse its strength or clothe its neck with a flowing mane? It paws fiercely, rejoicing in its strength, and charges into the fray. It laughs at fear, afraid of nothing" (Job 39:19, 21).

God defines the immensity of his being, though he does not infer we should never question circumstances. We would be remiss not to approach God in our attempts to understand suffering just as Job's dialog with God reflects a need for his own understanding. We will not understand all aspects of suffering on this side of Heaven, but we hold to our faith that God's love will stand in the gap for us.

Job answers God. "I know that you can do all things; no purpose of yours can be thwarted. Surely I spoke of things I did not understand, things too wonderful for me to know" (Job 42:2, 3). Ultimately Job's hope was realized, and his losses were restored seven times over. Through unimaginable suffering, Job refused to surrender his hope and faith in God. Through trials of our own, as we question our own personal suffering, we can choose to trust God for what we do not understand, allowing him to strengthen and guide us into a future of hope.

Falling

Responding to a page from the patient advocate, I walk toward the emergency department knowing only that the patient is critical. In the family waiting area, I find a pretty brunette with blue eyes swollen from crying. She reaches out with both hands and clasps both of mine. After quick introductions, I take a seat beside her and she says, "We pray together every morning for my husband and his crew. He won't leave for work before we pray for their safety. One of his men called out this morning, so he was in a hurry. He wasn't even *supposed* to be there today. When he was walking out the door, he looked back at me over his shoulder and said, 'I already prayed.'" Slowly shaking her head, she says, "I'm so thankful he told me he did."

We sit and wait for information that can bring hope or despair. As we wait, the patient's brother enters the waiting room, anxious, though focused. One glance tells me maintaining control is his comfort zone, tailored business suit, perfectly matched tie, every hair in place. He comforts his brother's wife then excuses himself to make a call. I silently wonder if the patient is like him, and as though she has read my mind, the patient's wife says, "My husband isn't anything like his brother. He's just as smart but he always has to be outdoors." I picture him in jeans, a work shirt and gloves, on that roof three stories above the ground, perhaps performing a job he normally does not do every day, to keep his company going, ensuring there is no slack.

We pray every day for the safety of my husband and his crew. What happened? What is this faithful wife thinking? What if they had prayed together, prayed harder, prayed differently? What if they had not prayed at all? Do we worship a God ready to punish if we miss a beat? If I did not believe God is merciful, I could not do my job; yet, illness, tragedy, and death are not easily understood. Our world is hazardous, full of imperfections and injustices. Our world, amazing, exciting, and dangerous, offers opportunities only an omnipotent perfect God could create. In our world, we encounter abundant life and the pain of death and all things in between. "In this world you will have tribulation but take courage; I have overcome the world" (John 16:33 NASB).

The patient is airlifted to a well-known hospital in a larger city nearby with excellent neurosurgeons. I say goodbye to his lovely wife as she quickly prepares for the trip as well, communicating with her family. As is often the case, I do not know the outcome, nor do I need to. I have completed my portion of this family's journey, and I know the God who continues with them has held this family in His hands all along . . .

27

Sacred Ground

I walk into the room expecting to see the family who has requested chaplain support, but all is silent except the patient's quiet breathing. Guessing they have taken a break, I sit in the bedside chair, pulling out a business card, turning it over to write a note to the patient's family, "I am sorry to have missed you . . ."

I look up at the patient who, except for my knowledge of the situation, would appear only to be sleeping. I stare into her face, positioned toward me on the pillow. I whisper a prayer for her, and almost wonder if I have invaded her privacy. I have entered without her knowledge, and in near proximity gaze into her face, though she has never met me. I wonder who she is, who has loved her, and if she had the choice, whether she would want me here. I wonder if she would reach out her frail hand if she was able. Whether we would have soft conversation about her grandchildren, and those things her wisdom has gathered and taught her to share. My heart is grievous that I cannot know her just a little—that I cannot offer her verbal comfort. I watch as she struggles harder to breath. I marvel that dying can seem at times as difficult as being born.

I write a note for the family and look over into the patient's face once more. Goodbye to you, sweet woman, whom I never knew. I believe we will meet again.

Menagerie of Lives

I return my page to acknowledge a request for pastoral care in ICU. The patient's husband stands beside her bed, and she appears to be sleeping. As I approach, her husband extends his hand, and following introductions, he begins to relate the story of his life since two a.m. He concludes with the fact that his wife is doing poorly, and he is essentially staying at the hospital. She is waking up, and we interact only briefly since she is in pain. I notify her nurse and return to let them know help is on the way. We pray at their request, and I leave to allow the patient privacy as her pain subsides.

As I walk through the unit, I see a middle-aged man standing beside a patient who is intubated, young. The nurse rushes in to check a monitor, and I make a mental note to check on them later.

The ER is busy. One physician is addressing a family asking why their mother has died. "You know what your mother's lifestyle has been," he said, sounding frustrated, his hands slightly animated. "How is it you wonder what happened?" As I come closer, I see the physician wears a sad expression. "Look," he says to the family, "I know this is painful, but the 'whys' are a lifetime deep. Maybe you can talk with the chaplain, find some peace. I'm sorry for your loss." My heart is heavy for everyone involved. This burdened family has little to say. They *do* know of their mother's past choices and drug addiction. They offer that they tried to help her, attempted to intervene though she always returned to her addictions. I have learned, no matter the love or intentions of family or friends, the addict must *want* help, must want to find other meaning in life. Free will is a strong factor when it comes to making choices. It can be marvelous and creative or destructive and devastating.

And always, there is guilt. It is a hell of a thing when friends and family suffer again at the end-result of an addiction turned deadly. Having fought the good fight, families are only human, and at times burn-out is inevitable. I witness nurses, especially recent graduates, grieve when their patients have few or no visitors at the end stages of addiction. They find it difficult to understand in their fresh hopeful hearts what it has taken me years of walking these halls to understand; addicts can exhaust friends and family, often to the point families make their own difficult choices. Being consistently depleted of emotional and mental energy, the human spirit's inward sensitivity struggles to cope and understand. Distance or dissolve may occur between family members and the source of the threat to a healthy personal life. This seemingly reasonable choice may result in relief and a return to *normalcy*, but seldom forgetting. When there is death due to addiction, loving friends and family are once again thrust into emotional stress, even deep regret and guilt. Later chapters address this emotional turmoil and other *what ifs* resulting from occurrences in my own life.

I notice the ED nurses attempting to calm a patient, a young combative male. The strong odor of alcohol alerts me this visit should occur at a later time. As a chaplain resident, I learned most individuals hospitalized for alcohol withdrawal or drug overdose do not remember initial conversations which transpire while chemical agents are present in their systems. My CPE supervisor encouraged student chaplains to refer these patients to mental health experts whenever possible for evaluation and support prior to spiritual care interactions. Nurses often make this determination well, providing staff the opportunity to receive information and background from psychiatric disciplines prior to intervention. Later, when the chemical has abated, staff can interact with the patient to consider resources as well as further needs, spiritual and otherwise. Prayerfully, the patient will be open to assistance which could determine a path to healing.

28

Denial . . .

The ED secretary tells me that the woman in bed one should be given priority. She is thirty-five, a medical assistant student doing an externship at a nearby facility. This afternoon, she decided her life is not worth living. She greets me with aloofness, informing me, "I am fine."

I gaze into hazel eyes. "Depends upon your definition of fine," I reply.

With a hint of defiance, she tells me, "I've never done anything like this. My life is good." I allow a beat of silence after her statement, and she begins to talk through her present situation. After a lengthy separation from her husband, they are going through a divorce. Because she has moved in with her new boyfriend, her husband is threatening to file for full custody of their daughter. The young woman adds the boyfriend has a *quick* temper. Her words hang there for a moment as involuntary tears roll down her cheeks. It is as though she is saddened by hearing her own words. Life is *not* good, not even close.

The ER doc enters. Having trained in suicide survivor counseling, he tells her whatever has caused her to be depressed to the point of attempting self-harm should be treated medicinally immediately. He leaves no gray area for therapy alone. The physician enters a behavioral health consult, to include an in-depth psychological evaluation. She has survived a desperate moment, and the hope is her sense of vulnerability will present a willingness to receive help. The physician completes a quick physical exam, engages in brief conversation with the patient, and leaves.

The patient continues sharing her perspective. She tells me she is in love with her boyfriend and does not want to leave him. She expresses love for her daughter as well, saying she does not want to lose her, though she is fearful of her husband's legal action. When I ask about family support, she offers that her mother is across the country and her sister lives in another state, although they talk. I inquire whether she and her boyfriend communicate well, and she says, "No." She says she does not like to talk which makes her boyfriend mad. I ask if she thinks counseling will help. She asks, "Who?" I indicate, *her, them, everyone.* She says her boyfriend would never go to counseling. I tell her it is important to consider what is best for her and her daughter. She says she will.

I offer to pray with this young woman, and she shares she has not been in church in years, that she is unworthy to pray. I reply she is covered by the same grace that covers us all and extend my hand. She takes it, and together we pray about many things—her life, her relationships, and the daughter for whom she will provide an example, prayerfully one of fortitude.

29

Deepest Places

I wake up and hold still, as though this will lessen the impact of the senseless death of one of our nurses. I attempt to focus on the tasks of my day off, but the laundry draped across my arm cannot distract the emotions struggling to surface. From her colleagues, the accounts echo in my head. "She didn't come to work, and she wouldn't do that, just not show up," they said. Three of her friends, comrades in nursing, drove to her home where they found she had been violently murdered. They were beyond devastated, beyond traumatized. They told me, "You could follow where she tried to run. There was blood . . . Her handprints were on the back of the front door. We can't stand it, hearing her scream in our minds. None of us knows what to do."

I walk out to the Magnolia tree. A magnificent old tree, it will be cut down when the highway widens. How many years has it grown here? I take a couple of its blossoms inside, placing them on my table where the fragrance fills the room.

A life which has brought joy and significance, now gone. A selfless young woman caring for countless others, a mother with a little daughter, thankfully at the sitters when her mother's life was taken. It will take time to sift through thoughts of this senselessness, years for the nurses, perhaps lifetimes. They lamented, "She was such a good person. Why? Why would anyone hurt her? She was an awesome nurse. You know those days when you get your patient list and think, 'Great,' because it's the patient nobody wants? She never turned over a shift like that, in a negative way. She could get assigned a patient who was puking, mean-spirited, it didn't matter. When she gave her shift report she would say, 'You know that Mr. Smith is so sweet.' She made us all want to be better nurses."

My best galfriend comes by and we sit outside under the Magnolia and talk about when our kids were little and laugh out loud. I tell her, "You know that potato salad you like? Come on in and I'll make you some." She looks at me questioningly.

"That takes too long," she says.

"Come on," I tell her. So, I make fresh potato salad with herbs she likes, and she eats it while it is still warm. She is alive and here with me, and this moment is one I can have with her. She hugs me while I wash dishes. At times, knowledge that the years are limited makes them so precious.

My fellow-chaplain calls. We have long bonded over discussions of illness and death, connecting our spirits and our work. This is different, and we search for words. Our hearts and empathy ache for her family, her little daughter. If this grief can be solaced, it will be Christ the King who sustains this family, this staff, this community. It will take time for the discovery that her killer chose her house at random. A would-be robbery, he robbed the world of a giver.

"For I am persuaded that neither death nor life, nor angels nor principalities nor powers, nor things present nor things to come, nor height nor depth, nor any other thing, shall be able to separate us from the love of God which is in Christ our Lord" (Romans 8:38-39 NKJV).

No depth can separate us.

30

A Beautiful Mind . . .

I walk into the room where a young couple is lying together in the hospital bed. As they face one another, his hand is on the side of her face, and he gently pushes back her hair. When they see me, they smile, and he casually gets up, as though all patients and spouses naturally cohabitate the hospital bed. This makes me smile too because it is so unabashed. She looks at him and speaks first, "What was it we wanted to ask the chaplain?" He begins . . .

"I was wondering about the journeys of Joshua, and why he aligned himself with the prophets as they were not hallowed, although they were viewed as such. They were often self-appointed and arrogant. There must be a theological answer to why he configured his followers to stand as they did with the prophets, but I have not been able to figure that out. Also, was the Battle of Jericho purely strategic on God's part, because I see it as such a spiritually empowered force of good against evil . . ."

Initially, I believe he wants to engage in theological sparing. It takes another ten minutes before I realize I am wrong. His mind is in a spiritual quandary, and he is all over the place. It is as though he is having a biblical conversation with himself, struggling, justifying, searching the scriptures. I begin to see his scriptural genius. He knows and cites biblical scripture largely accurately, perhaps better than my college professors—the characters, their dilemmas, as well as God's direction to them or comments on them.

His initial questions have been absorbed by the wealth of information which followed, and I find myself engrossed in this man's mental status. Engaging in further conversation with both the patient and the man I discover to be her fiancée, I gradually realize he appears challenged discussing simpler things. I catch the patient's expression, at moments akin to concern or even frustration. I ask the man if he has plans for his gifts. He shares he has gone to college, though he did not finish, adding he experienced boredom and difficulty concentrating. He says he does plan to further pursue his education. I tell him he should.

As we share a prayer and bid farewell, I am certain I will long remember this man and the woman by his side, recalling the uniqueness of a beautiful mind.

31

A Sudden Storm

An Alpha Alert is called overhead for the emergency department. A sudden storm just ended, and I mistakenly assume the alert is the result of an accident. I walk down the corridor with little anxiety, just as I have responded hundreds of times. As I near the unit normally ignited with activity, there is a solemn hush—a sign an emergency out of the norm has been wheeled through those big double doors. Sad eyes are reflected in sidebar doctorial conversations.

It is summertime. My mind goes to the beach, and I am not wrong. Our beautiful city perched on the edge of the earth draws many vacationers yearly. The family has traveled from New York with their two kids, seven and eight, a daughter and son. The father, thirty-seven, became disoriented while playing on the beach with them, then sitting down on a towel beside his wife, he suffered a fatal heart attack. Bewildered and distraught, his wife is making every attempt to remain strong for their children. The couple traveled here with friends, the wife a pediatrician, strong and supportive in this nightmare.

This patient was previously healthy and active. His wife asks, "Why?" The ED physicians tell her it will take time to attempt to uncover the cause. She relates, as though in a fog, how they woke up in a beautiful hotel room, excited about activities they planned around the beach and the children. She tells us he was an amazing father and husband. A tall man with tousled reddish hair and freckles, she touches his hands, his face. She tells him, "We didn't get to say goodbye." She does not prevent the children from hearing, from experiencing the sadness. She does not discourage them from coming near, looking longingly at their father, needing his arms around them, and being with him in the end.

The family and their friends occupy this cubical of our hospital. Slow, devastated, questioning tears fall. We are helpless in a remedy, present in prayer, sharing disbelief, holding hands, and embracing adults as well as children too young to totally comprehend this sudden horrendous event. This is what we are ordained to do, where we were destined to be in these terrible moments. "Weep with those who weep . . . Mourn with those who mourn . . ." (Romans 12:15 NKJV, NIV).

32

Right Here Right Now

I walk into the room of a patient who asked to be placed on "suicide watch." A complete psychiatric evaluation will be implemented. He asked to see a chaplain as well, and I introduce myself. He smiles a thoughtful smile, and it occurs to me he was perhaps expecting a male. I take a seat beside his bed, and after initial conversation, he has not mentioned the reason for his request. I ask, "Why did you ask to be placed on suicide watch?" He looks down, and I add, "It's alright, we seek options to get out of a crappy situation sometimes. I am not here to judge you, but I think I can help you put things into perspective. I just want to ask, what feels so badly that you want to escape?"

"I always feel I've let my family down."

I ask, "In what way?"

He replies, "My wife is never happy."

"How long has she been unhappy?"

"A long time, I can't remember."

"What would happen to her if you took your life?"

"She would say, 'See, I told you he was a loser.'"

"Your children?" Silence. I continue, "Let me share something I'm certain of. Whether or not your wife or your children would miss you or be sad, suicide passes a legacy of pain to anyone you care about. Whatever you are feeling, you probably care about someone in this life, right?"

"Yes, I love my children with all my heart."

"Then if you love your children and anyone else, suicide isn't the answer. Never. You would be gone, yet those you love would be left to struggle with questions about your death for the rest of their lives. Do you understand?"

"Yeah, I see that."

"Sometimes a part of the suicidal thought process is wanting someone else to pay for your pain and struggles. Have you experienced that in your thoughts of suicide?"

"I have. Mostly my wife, but I didn't think it through about my kids."

"You don't want defeat. You sound as though you have had enough of feeling defeated."

He smiles a weary smile. "You got that right."

"Alright, then you have to figure out a path to victory—a path to a better way."

He shakes his head. "I don't know where to start."

"Right here, right now, sir. You start right here . . ."

Years into the future, I will deeply lament I never had the opportunity to speak these words of reason to my own father.

33

The Scent of Christ

I t is nearing the end of my shift. Before leaving, I check on the wife of a patient for whom a Code Blue was called when his heart stopped earlier today. All is well in this moment.

There is a new referral, and the physician has written a note that his patient recently lost her husband. The nurse tells me her patient is dreading going home to an empty house, giving me the patient's denomination, Greek Orthodox. These are the nurses I am continually thankful for, amazingly compassionate and aware of her patient's religious denomination.

As I open the door, a kind face looks back at me, the possible history of a stroke evidenced by a slight drooping of her right cheek. She smiles, and I introduce myself. I explain our medical staff wants to make sure she has the support she needs, that I am sadly aware she recently lost her husband. She begins her story . . . Forty-five years together, a son, and a good life. The patient tells me her husband began drawing closer to God a couple of months before he died in her arms. She recalls that he crossed himself frequently, he lit a candle, and talked of God. His wife shares her happiness concerning her husband's renewal of faith, exclaiming, "Thank God; I thank Jesus!" In her beautiful thick Greek accent.

"Yes, thank God," I agree. "What comfort this must lend you now."

"He died in my arms." She stretches open her left arm and places her right hand where his head must have rested. We sit in silence for a moment.

"You will see your husband again. God will orchestrate that beautiful moment." We pray and chat a bit. I tell her I will see her in Heaven one day as well and meet her husband.

"You smell like . . ." She uses a word I do not hear clearly, but I know it is good, as she is smiling, so I smile back.

"I'm sorry, I don't understand," I tell her.

"Yeshua," she repeats. "I smell the scent of Christ on you." I am caught off guard. She continues, "I smelled it when you came in. Can't you? I can; it is all around us." I am speechless. I place my hand over my heart because I know He is here.

"God goes before me," I tell her. I open my mouth to say more, but it is not necessary. We say our goodbyes and I tell her we will meet again. I am filled with awe of who God is, although we understand only a small part. Humility overwhelms me.

"Now we see through a glass darkly, but then face to face: now I know in part; but then I shall know even as I am known" (1 Corinthians 13:12 KJV).

The Sheep of His Pasture

When a mother sheep looks for her lamb, she can find it even though most lambs look alike. Whether there are twenty or two hundred lambs in the pasture, every ewe can tell her lamb by its scent. Likewise, when each baby is born, he or she has a unique scent. A newborn baby has a special scent of which only his or her parents may be aware.

My grandmother referred to Christ at times as, "The Lamb that was slain." With her high school education, my grandmother knew scripture better than most theologians. "Worthy is the Lamb who was slain to receive power and riches and wisdom, and strength, and honor and glory and blessing! And every creature which is in Heaven and on the earth and under the earth and such as are in the sea, and all that are in them, I heard saying: 'Blessing and honor and glory and power be to Him who sits on the throne, and to the Lamb, forever and ever!'" (Revelation 5:11-12 NKJV).

Representing God's perfect love, His only Son is known as the perfect Lamb. Through God's grace, we not only come to recognize the scent of Christ; we come to give off the scent of Christ. "Now, thanks be to God who always leads us in triumph in Christ, and through us diffuses the fragrance of His knowledge in every place. For we are to God the fragrance of Christ" (2 Corinthians, 2:14, 15 NKJV). God not only catches the scent of Christ *on us,* He also reflects His love to others *through us.* It is in our hearts, in our souls, and this is the way God views our being; we give off the scent of His only Son, Jesus Christ, our risen Savior and Lord.

34

You Must Stay

His father is a successful business developer. His mother is accustomed to being heard. And he is losing his well-fought battle with acute myeloid leukemia. The patient is only twenty-nine, and his wife of three years is quiet and exhausted. As we stand outside the young man's room, the physician addresses his condition. Though the patient's wife is present, the physician directs most of his update toward the parents. I call his attention to her, "You've met the patient's wife, sir?"

"Yes, we've met." The physician replies. Though he makes a more concerted effort to address the young woman, her in-laws answer him back. Taking center stage, they are now discussing end-of-life decisions and comfort care. When I inquire about the medical power of attorney, the patient's wife says she remains in that capacity and her in-laws are helping her make decisions. Knowing the patient is currently awake and somewhat oriented, I ask, "What does your husband want?"

"Not to be in pain," she says.

"We are *not* ready to make a decision regarding comfort care," the patient's mother replies. "He is being kept comfortable, and his father and

I don't want to give up aggressive treatment," she adds.

"What about a bedside conference with your son, his wife, and the physicians?" I ask.

"We don't want to stress him more," his mother says. "He has been through enough."

"What do you think? Are you in agreement?" I ask the patients wife.

"He would want to continue to be included, but . . ." she offers as her voice softly trails off. Both parents look somewhat perplexed.

I offer, "Would he want you to hear his thoughts?"

"He should be included," the father states. "He is still able." The attending physician suggests we set up a family meeting with his patient, including his oncologist.

The young patient is military and stoic. "I am tired," he says. "I don't want to continue aggressive treatment when my life is going to end in a short time regardless. I just want to be with my family." Tears roll down his wife's face, though his mother does not seem aware. His mother urges her son to continue treatment, "Perhaps something will be discovered tomorrow . . ." she says. "We do not want to give up too soon."

"Mom," the patient looks at her, his shaky hand reaching out to hers. "If we had given up months ago, it still would not have been too soon. We have fought hard. You have all fought for me and now it is time to let go. To let me go." She crumbles on his chest, sobbing the throaty cry of a heartbroken mother. His father is silent with his own trail of tears. He tugs at his wife's arm.

"Let's give them some time," he says, referring to his son and daughter-in-law. His wife is resistant.

"I am right outside the door," she says.

"I know, Mom," he answers. As his parents go, his wife steps closer. They take one another's hands, and he looks into her eyes. "I don't want to die, but you're strong. You've fought like hell with me, and you will be alright," he says. She softly agrees and lowers her head as he pulls her toward him and kisses her hair. As she lifts her face to his, I quietly walk out.

As the days pass, the patient's parents share feelings of helplessness and despair. They continue to remain the more vocal spokespersons, and the patient's wife seems comfortable with this unfolding.

As much as we may attempt to prepare ourselves for death, it still delivers an emotional and mental shock. We anticipate the pain of departure as best we can, though it is not quite enough to transition us from seeing the spirit within the person we love, to the spirit's clear absence. A person immediately looks different, a phenomenon I have witnessed and pondered many times. No matter how ill the patient, the swift departure of the spirit upon death often leaves loved ones in an impactful place of grief.

Just as before her son's passing, his mother remains most vocal afterwards. Her husband and daughter-in-law, though weeping, are quiet in their mourning. The patient's mother and wife remain at the bedside long after his father leaves the room. As the patient's wife takes a few steps toward the door, his mother pulls her back. "You must stay," she almost commands. "You can't leave, just talk to him and tell him how much you've loved him." His wife's painful expression says everything. I gently put my arm around the patient's mother.

"You're his mother," I softly say, desiring not to diminish this moment. "His wife has her own grief, and only she can decide what that looks like." I turn around and quietly walk the patient's wife out the door. She looks at me with a sad brief smile. "He was right, you know," I tell her. "You are strong, and you will be alright." After a brief hug, I leave to allow this family the privacy they need in the unfolding of their grief, to say goodbye in their own personal ways.

The hospital room is powerfully significant in the scope of illness and death. Memories will linger from here throughout lifetimes. The words of a chaplain during heartbreak and emotional disarray can help or ring hollow. And the presence of a chaplain, no matter how well meaning, can be supportive *or* invasive. The sensitivity of all hospital staff and visitors is vital in their involvement with patients and families during this vulnerable time.

"To console those who morn in Zion, To give them beauty for ashes. The oil of joy for mourning. The garment of praise for the spirit of heaviness . . ." (Isaiah 61:3 NKJV).

35

Bearing Burdens, Allowing Space

Paul says whatever state he is in, he has learned to be content. Grief, in the short term, does not usually produce feelings of contentment. Death is anything but comforting. Yet, acknowledging God's presence and power may prevent us from taking everything solely upon our shoulders. The burden of illness, death, or grief is not meant to be carried by any one man or woman. When we acknowledge God's power, we share our burdens with an almighty God and access his strength for help during life events that do not work out as we had planned—those heartaches we do not want or could not foresee. "Bear ye one another's burdens . . ." (Galatians 6:2 KJV)

As a support person or caregiver, a desire to comfort should not outweigh the needs of a patient or family. If it does, an intrusion upon a sacred place where we are neither needed nor even especially welcome can occur. A chaplain, clergy, friend, or support person must be astute enough to recognize when to back away. The patient and family will give off recognizable indicators of their need to privately draw together to effectively cope and may express this verbally or non-verbally. Identify and allow space. Sensitivity to these indicators is always a positive attribute of the best supporter or caregiver.

Comfort Zones

Unwilling to speak up at times as a chaplain resident, my clinical pastoral education director advised, "Jan, don't be afraid to rock the boat." I was slightly insulted, as I took pride in the calm demeanor sometimes commented on by others. It took years of a chaplain's walk to understand our strengths are also our weaknesses, though God can help us balance them.

Often empathetic and understanding, *people pleasers* desire to encourage and assist others. The flip side is, to make people feel good, people pleasers hesitate to point out the negative or any need to do things differently, even if change is needed. "Better are the wounds of a friend than the flattery of an enemy" (Proverbs 27:6). As in the classic tale, *The Emperor's New Clothes*, at times, everyone agrees all is fine when all is not fine. As an encourager, I sometimes hesitate to speak up regarding issues which can and should be resolved. I like to remain in my comfort zone.

As with most engrained personality traits, lending encouragement has been part of my psyche since I was a child. When my parents argued, I learned that calmness and positivity would help facilitate resolve between them. While I appreciate the strength of positivity, as an adult, I must deal with the flip side of this strength, which is a weakness of accepting what should be remedied. Through God's guidance and continuing spiritual growth, I learned to venture outside my comfort zone to speak up when all is not well, but it is, at times, challenging. By incorporating assertiveness into my skillset when needed, it has become more natural. Still, I will forever be far happier sharing what is right rather than what is wrong.

Continually in the process of growth and assimilation, the challenges we face increase our awareness of challenges *others* face. Looking to Christ as mentor, pointing others to him as theirs, we unite to experience growth and change rather than judging one another. It is exciting to discover what God will do with us next—strengths, weaknesses, issues, and all!

36

Psalm 37

The daughter of my best friend calls at five in the morning. "Aunt Janet," she says, "My mom is at the hospital. She's had some sort of *episode*. Can you come?" I get a few details, mainly that her mom felt weak and almost collapsed the previous night, but insisted she just needed some sleep. In my mind, I think about the hard time I will give her, getting everyone up early. In my heart, I am concerned she may have suffered a mild CVA or even a heart attack. I am familiar with the hospital where she has been taken and know she is in good hands. I am not even in a particular rush as I dress and head out. As I exit the hospital elevator, her daughter meets me. "I'm so glad you're here," she says, looking at me with huge blue eyes. Then she asks a question I will never forget. "Aunt Janet, what does 'fixed and dilated mean?'"

Oh God, oh God, I think. I say, "Honey, it is not good." We walk along the corridor to ICU where her mother, my precious confidant, lies hooked up to everything that no longer helps. I notice her ultra-feminine hands, her nails; they are perfect, and it seems all I can focus on. Her daughter is asking me questions the physicians have already asked her regarding taking her mother off life support. This cannot be happening . . .

I recall a conversation with my precious friend before my son was born regarding Psalm 37:4, "Delight yourself in the Lord, and He shall give you the desires of your heart." I had taken it at face value, asking God for a son after three daughters. My friend had looked deeper. "I think it means God will place His desires in our hearts," she said. "The desires which are best for us and most glorifying to God."

Her daughter tells me, "I felt her spirit leave. Mom isn't here."

We met when our children were babies, and before two of mine were born. New to the neighborhood, I walked two houses down to meet the gal another neighbor described as "sweet and friendly." Her warmth put me at ease immediately, while her little daughter bounced off the couch. The same daughter with whom I now stand.

I once attended a seminar during which a short film highlighted "perspective." A photographer illustrated through his camera how the same object can look entirely different, depending upon the angle of the lens. From all angles, my spiritual friend was beautifully photogenic. I viewed many perspectives of a deep and abiding relationship for twenty-one years. Extremely witty and forthright, the spirit God placed in her was also very loving. She would walk in, place her hands on each side of your face, look at you close in the eyes, and speak sweet positive words. She had a personal way of making others feel *valued.* And she did value others greatly, and she did let them know. I thank God that each of my children experienced her love. She left a spirit of sweetness that lingered, even after she had gone.

My friend spoke of our Lord Jesus Christ in the same personal way she showed His love to others. She sometimes had visions of what she believed was to be, or of what was to be God's will. In the year prior to her death, she mentioned things that neither of us understood at the time. She shared with me how she envisioned herself in beautiful clothes, surrounded by riches. She once described in detail her long flowing white ensemble. Another time, she dreamed of being in a castle, surrounded by others caring for her needs. Because of our earthly nature, we attempted to give her visions and dreams earthly meaning. Because we were girlfriends, we giggled a little. But now, she partakes in those things we only spoke of. She now sees what our eyes had not seen and hears what our ears had not heard regarding what God had prepared for her.

My friend and I once sat in my office looking through a LifeNet album of those who had donated organs upon their passing. The photographs of such regular people, young and old, were heart-wrenching as well as mesmerizing. She asked if she might take the album home for a few days to finish looking through it. We never once considered her picture would be entered in this album, portraying a beautiful young woman, intelligent, giving, loving, and kind, taken from those who loved her before we were ready to let her go.

Ironically, my friend sent out a Thanksgiving email only days before her death. "Do not let your hearts be troubled . . . Trust in God, trust also in me. In my house are many mansions, if it were not true, I would have told you . . ." Words of Christ from John. And from Philippians, "Do not be anxious about anything, but in everything, by prayer and petition, with thanksgiving, present your requests to God, and the peace of God, which transcends all understanding, will guard your hearts and your minds in Christ Jesus." At times, the peace of God during pain must surpass understanding. In the email, my dear friend asked for forgiveness from her friends and family for any hurts she had ever caused. I thought it *deep* for a Thanksgiving email, but it was perfect for a transcending goodbye.

My youngest daughter wrote: "I am mistaken because I always took you for granted. For a person like you, Heaven should be an understatement. Paradise, eternal bliss with unlimited manicures and laughter, is where I hope to meet you someday. I hope you watch as I get married, and as I look into the face of my baby. I hope you watch and whisper the words to lullabies in my ear as I rock them to sleep, with the same singsong voice you had. Our memories are priceless, and you have blessed my life in so many ways . . . I love you, and you will never be forgotten."

Each of us kept our own personal favorite snapshot of my dear friend's presence in our lives. Paul summed her up beautifully. "Love . . . suffers long and is kind . . . Rejoices in the truth . . . Bears all things, believes all things . . . hopes all things . . . Endures all things. Love never fails. For now, we see in a mirror, dimly, but then face to face. Now I know in part, but then I shall know, just as I am known. And now abide faith, hope, love—these three. But the greatest of these is love" (Excerpts from I Cor. Ch. 13). Thank you, sweet girlfriend, confidant, my spiritual sister, for sharing your precious time with me. Thank you for sharing God's love with us. May God watch between us and thee until we meet again. I am so thankful I made you potato salad.

Heaven's Door

The rose appears to bow her head,
    Admitting you are gone.
I look out o'er the early dew
    And hear the dove's low moan.
A world in testimony,
    Confessions of this grief
And lo, the Weeping Willow
    Yields forth her saddest leaf.
For none can be requited
    From soft witness of the tear,
Nor quench the deepest yearning
    We might look to find you here.
Though we, Dear Sister, would not bring
    You back from heaven's door.
For though we love with heart and soul,
    Your Father loves thee more.

Jan

37

God *is* Good

A s a child, my parents taught me a prayer to say at mealtime. Many children around the world may have learned, "God is great, God is good, God we thank you for our food," or other variations of this prayer.

I have now been a chaplain for many years. I could not have remained in this line of work if God had not strengthened and increased my faith. I have learned first-hand the prayer my parents taught me is true. God *is* great, God *is* good. God is for us. "If God is for us, who can be against us?" (Romans 8:31). This belief is sometimes challenged in ministry to the sick and dying, as it can be challenged in our personal lives as well. The question, "How could God let this happen?" is the most difficult, if not the most dreaded question asked of clergy. Years of accompanying those experiencing unfair and devastating illness and circumstances have caused me to deeply explore this question. While we will not understand all things on this side of the "glass," the development of a personal conviction regarding suffering has brought me peace in ministry and in my personal spiritual life. "Now we see through a glass darkly, but then face to face: now I know in part; but then I shall know even as I am known" (1 Corinthians 13:12 KJV).

When God spun the worlds into motion, we were at the center of the universe he created, "a little lower than the angels" (Psalm 8:5). Free will was bestowed upon us, and God pronounced it *good* (Genesis 1:31). The *only* way God could create us perfectly, however, was to give us the choice to be *imperfect*. Through his divine mercies, we remain inherently good.

If we could somehow program our own children, born perfect and innocent, to do everything right, behave in the ways we dictate, and cause us no worry—though they would haves no choices of their own—would we? Most loving parents would never short circuit the experiences and character of their children in this way, even if this were possible. This *was* possible when God created us, yet he chose to give us free will, our own will.

Humankind took the gift of free choice and *recreated* God's perfect world. Becoming incongruent with God's will resulted in a cost to civilization. At the point of creation, perhaps we possessed one hundred percent of our brain power. As we made choices less than wise and beneficial, we short-circuited ourselves in the process. We brought dissension, sin, imperfection, illness, and evil into our perfect world, yet we blame God for unfairness and atrocities, asking how *he* could let these terrible things continue. Our choices resulted in lessening perfection and increasing chaos. Only Christ, God's own Son, when given free will, chose to use it to do the Father's will. Thankfully for us, Christ is our grace.

We continue to make mistakes and pray God will intervene. Lovingly and mercifully, he often does. Yet how often would God need to intervene to change the course of events before we lost our free will. If God corrected every incorrect choice, eventually we would lose accountability and perhaps our integrity. Enabling our children to make less than good decisions by consistently bailing them out is not conducive to raising strong individuals. And while God does not always deliver us from our decisions or the suffering we experience, he does show great compassion and mercy, just as we do for our own children. The sacrifice of Christ upon the cross paid for our mistakes, and with our free will, we choose to accept this gift of love or reject it. Christ has said, "In this world, you will have tribulation. Be of good cheer, I have overcome the world" (John 16:33 NASB).

Our imperfect world, its fears, anxieties, and turmoil, has been overcome by God's perfect love. We can present our pain to him and trust we will receive help in every facet of our lives. My work involves poor prognoses and good ones, sudden changes, death, and miracles, including birth. It involves patients, family, and staff, and it involves my spirit, even when it is doubtful or broken. My work is infinitely rewarding, even when circumstances are unfair, wrong, or out of control. I acclimate to the chaos, because I know God will enable me to represent his love in the middle of it. "Fear not, for I am with you; Be not dismayed, for I am your God. I will strengthen you, Yes I will help you, I will uphold you with My righteous right hand" (Isaiah 41:10 NKJV). "God is *for* us. And if God is for us, who can be against us?" (Romans 8:31 NIV). Not even we ourselves.

Yesterday and Today

I sit with a cancer patient who has battled her original diagnosis for years, and whose current prognosis had taken a turn for the worse. She shares with me that she experienced strong faith following her original diagnosis. She tells me how she, like her father, believed she would overcome this *medical monster*. "But now," she says, "I am afraid. The worst part is that my fear causes me to believe my faith is weak." She is experiencing emotional trauma because she does not believe she is handling the situation in a *spiritually appropriate manner.*

I listen to this lovely person pour her heart out and ask, "You believe being afraid of this disease and its consequences equates your fear with weak faith?" When she acknowledges, I ask whether biblical advice on fear helps. She says it makes her feel guilty as she is not able to receive the spiritual strength to overcome her fear. I share, "The reason the Bible offers advice on fear is because God knows we will experience fear. You are afraid because what you are experiencing is scary."

"There are times I trust God," she said. "I experience moments of faith and humility, but this disease is seriously worse every day. I become uncertain what to feel and that leads back to fear and doubt. And no matter how much faith I have, death is a place I will go with God alone. No one else I love is able to come."

No one else she loved was able to accompany her to Heaven. But on this side, they held her and sat with her during her hospitalizations. Her adult children and husband kept watch and comforted her fearfulness as well as one another's, as they eventually laid with her in the hospital bed. She passed amid abounding love and devotion, and I am certain, as she entered Heaven's boundaries, there were loving arms awaiting to welcome her there.

"Do not be afraid or dismayed because of this . . . for the battle is not yours, but God's. You will not need to fight in this battle. Position yourselves, stand still and see the salvation of the Lord, who is with you" (II Chronicles 20:15, 17 AB).

38

Homeless and Blessed

I first notice him standing on the corner of an intersection close to the hospital. He holds up a small brown cardboard sign which reads, "Homeless." The traffic light turns red as I approach the corner and, rolling down my window, I hand him a couple of dollars. In acknowledgement, he smiles and says, "Thank you." Later, I think of the reflections of pain and hope, even happiness, in his expression.

Over time, I make a habit of stopping for a brief chat with my friend when I am early for work. "It won't be this way in Heaven," I say to him. Our eyes meet and tear in the next silent seconds. Over the months, I share concerns with my colleagues and husband regarding my homeless acquaintance—the times he stands on the corner in the cold hoping to receive donations and food enough to get through another day. My family and co-workers get to know him vicariously through me, participating in acts of kindness orchestrated to lighten his load. Our department furnishes blankets and shirts, and on Christmas, we gift him with a camouflage backpack filled with mini toiletries, a fast-food gift card, and a small Bible.

It is a joy to deliver these offerings.

One especially frigid winter's day, I share my friend's presence at the corner with co-workers and we gather a small amount of money and a blanket. One co-worker rides along to deliver these things. As we hand our offerings out the window, I tell him, "Get out of the cold."

"I can now," he says.

"God bless you," I tell him.

"He always does," he replies. It has become habit to exchange these familiar words.

As we drive away, my co-worker comments, "There is something about him, isn't there? Something painful and kind. You can see it in his face." His face clearly captures his personal life experiences—the goodness and pain, as someone who has been broken but who is not finished. A palpable vulnerability shades his demeanor, as does a strength.

After a four-year acquaintance, I am familiar with my homeless friend's determination, as well as some of his dreams. He carries a painful past, a present faith, and a guarded hope. His shoulder-length dirty blond hair is usually neatly cut, compliments, I understand, of another homeless friend. He dresses in t-shirts, several of which my husband has given him, and jeans. I often wonder how a person like this, intelligent and kind-hearted, finds himself in this circumstance. One summer's day, I ask, "Would you be willing to share your life's story with me?" He agrees and we plan a time and place to talk. His story should be heard.

Over coffee, my friend shares he was born in 1965 at a Navy hospital. His parents' only son, he has two older sisters, and two younger, the youngest of whom is incarcerated. His father, who was in the Coast Guard, was abusive to him, though not toward his sisters. He adds that the relationships his sisters had with his parents seemed normal at the time, though they later became involved with drugs, as did he. When his parents separated after fifteen years of marriage, he left home at sixteen to live with friends of the family, ending his relationship with his father, who later died of alcohol-related causes. As a young adult, my friend shares, he began working in landscaping where he enjoyed much satisfaction.

Unfortunately, while working on a retaining wall, he experienced a back injury. The resulting pain led to drug dependence and brain seizures brought on by the medications, rendering him unable to work.

My friend confides he was once in love, though the three-year relationship ended when he was in his mid-thirties. Unable to find and hold down work due to his addiction and health issues, he eventually found himself homeless. An ED doc whom he befriended helped him through withdrawal, and the seizures stopped as well. He tells me a local landowner hired him to help with the upkeep of his property, allowing him to pitch a tent on the property as part of his payment. He continues the outside work, which he loves, but does not make enough to sustain more expensive living accommodations. My friend tells me a couple of acquaintances have tents nearby, though he essentially remains a loner because of addiction problems in the homeless community. He has filed unsuccessfully for disability and has ongoing legal applications filed in attempts to obtain government assistance and further resources. Spiritually, my friend tells me he often prays, a detail I already knew. Sometimes, though we try, life robs and beats us down.

When I asked about present relationships with family, my friend tells me his next oldest sister who married one of his long-time friends remains somewhat close and they keep in touch. When I asked about his mother, he says he saw her once in the past seven years. The pain of that moment shows clearly in his expression as he recounts that he was on the street corner when she passed by. As their eyes met, he says she turned her head away.

Whom Shall I Love?

"On one occasion, an expert in law stood up to test Jesus. 'Teacher,' he asked, 'What must I do to inherit eternal life?'

'What is written in the law?' He replied. 'How do you read it?'

He answered, 'Love the Lord your God with all your heart and with all your soul and with all your strength and with all your mind,' and, 'Love your neighbor as yourself.'

'You have answered correctly,' Jesus replied. 'Do this and you will live.'

But he wanted to justify himself, so he asked Jesus, 'And who is my neighbor?'

In reply, Jesus said: 'A *man* went down from Jerusalem to Jericho, when he was attacked by robbers. They stripped him of his clothes, beat him, and went away, leaving him half dead. A priest happened to be going down the same road, and when he saw the man, he passed by on the other side. So too, a Levite, when he came to the place and saw him, passed by on the other side. But a Samaritan, as he traveled, came to where the man was; and when he saw him, he took pity on him. He went to *him* and bandaged his wounds, pouring on oil and wine. Then he put the man on his own donkey, brought him to an inn, and took care of him. The next day, he took out two denarii, gave *them* to the innkeeper. 'Look after him,' he said, 'and when I return, I will reimburse you for any extra expense you may have.'

'Which of these three do you think was a neighbor to the man who fell into the hands of robbers?'

The expert in the law replied, 'The one who had mercy on him.'

Jesus told him, 'Go and do likewise'" (Luke 10:25-37 NIV).

"Good morning!" I call out to my friend.

"Good morning!" He responds with a smile.

"My husband made a good lunch for us today. Here's yours."

"Thank you!" He says and reaches into the passenger side car window to accept the bag. I grasp his hand.

"God bless you," I say.

"He always does." He replies. We smile and I drive away as the light changes. Each morning comes with a clarity all its own. "Through the Lord's mercies we are not consumed, Because His compassions fail not. They are new every morning" (Lamentations 3:22-23 NKJV). As should be ours.

39

"Pray with Me In-Between"

I am paged to the emergency department for a twenty-six-year-old man who has requested a chaplain. By the time I get there, he is in serious pain, writhing on the gurney and upset at a delay in receiving medications. The ER doc has a call in to the young man's pain specialist and hematologist. I learn he suffers from a form of sickle cell disease.

"Just pray with me in-between," he whispers. "In between the pain." The young man curses and apologizes, and screams out and curses, and prays, and so it continues for over an hour. This agonizing scenario is heartbreaking. *Finally*, the docs can coordinate treatment for this crisis. *Finally*, his tears and pleadings to God quieten, and he sleeps. I pray he sleeps the sweet carefree flight of freedom from this disease. I pray the arms of Christ cradle him as he rests his body and spirit. In-between.

Raging Winds

There is a place I sometimes go and bottomless the fall,
        So strong the tempest raging winds.
I reach to get a better hold and fear there waits no
saving grasp,
        And hear no one at all.
I try to speak an inward heart, it beating wildly on
        But utter only two sweet words,
        While to my knees, I slowly sink and wait to see if I
will live
        While all my faith is gone.
I hold the hands of those who weep, sooth brows on
dying faces
        They rest upon my soul at night.
Though this moment holds no peace for me as all my
vulnerability
        Is strewn to many places.
How can I be the helping one as death continues on?
        I cannot calm the raging ills,
As battles tear across my mind and I am lost or left
behind
        To search for signs of dawn.
Dear God, reach through disquieting thoughts to draw
us ever near,
        And grant us deep prevailing faith
To show reflections of Your grace,
        And cover us God, cover us with love that casts out
fear.

Jan Moberg

"There is no fear in love; but perfect love casts out fear . . ." (1 John 4:18 NKJV).

Gethsemane . . .
Watch with Me

Our faith is played out wherever we are and in whatever we do. One of the most important things any of us may ever do is to be with others a while. As a chaplain, I learned to give patients, families, and staff members a safe place to voice thoughts, fears, and hopes—a safe place to question life, and even faith. The personal beliefs, thoughts, and feelings used to cope with illness are many times shared and explored with those who are available and willing to listen. Life's review of failures and successes often surface during a long or serious illness. This thought process may generate grief, regret, hope, and even the forgiveness involved in the struggle of the human spirit to continue learning and growing until it departs this earthly dwelling.

It is beyond difficult to watch a fellow human being suffer or die. While chaplains are called to this ministry, families and loved ones are called here too. Serious illness as well as the dying process can produce unimaginable changes to the human body. Yet we see this painful process imagined. As the night was long in the garden of Gethsemane for those who kept watch for Christ, the night is long for those who keep watch presently for those in his or her charge.

This night, returning to my office, I bow my head and silently weep for lost lives, for dreams stolen by disease, and for the loneliness and grief of those left behind. I weep for the pain of separation and for the pain of togetherness, for what the years can do, and for those who will never have them. I weep for my inability to fully understand, or to give answers to those who are ill, and to those who care for the injured and the sick and dying. I cannot tarry in what seems a place without rationale, as we all must continue in the face of that which is not understood, in the presence of pain and suffering. Pain will inspire a search for solace. Even in the dark of exhaustion and confusion, we search for hope and understanding. That the end is not the end. ". . . That mortality may be swallowed up by life" (II Corinthians, 5:4 NKJV).

The immensity of human frailty and our insufficiencies to do enough create a realization that we will never be fully prepared for the travails of this world. We want to make it okay, but it is not. We want to make it make sense, but it does not. Only with God's strength may we combine our imperfections to find victory. Christ admonished his disciples in the Garden of Gethsemane, asking, "Can you not watch with me one hour?" And though they fell asleep, *he still wanted them there.* He still directed them, "Watch with me" (Matthew 26:40). And so, we continue to keep watch and wait with one another.

Beauty for Ashes

The family has asked for bedside prayer for their mother, eighty-eight, who has lapsed into unconsciousness. I walk to the unit finding the family has gone to eat and entering the room, sit in the bedside chair near the unresponsive patient. I speak to her quietly, telling her who I am. According to registration information, she is Baptist. Reading the 23rd Psalm, I pray a short prayer and sit, as so many times, wondering who she is and has been, who has loved her, and whether she has had a happy journey. She is at the end of life—peace reflected in her face. She will be another I will recognize when I enter Heaven. Perhaps she will ask, "Hey, weren't you the one who sat with me a while?" What a privilege to linger here on this sacred ground, whispering goodbye to a fellow traveler and believer, knowing this is only the beginning.

"Eye has not seen, nor ear heard, Nor have entered into the heart of man The things which God has prepared for those who love Him" (1 Corinthians 2:9 NKJV).

40

Pretty in Pink

I read an article which questions the necessity of yearly mammograms after a certain age, assuming previous mammograms have yielded normal results. Considering my history of yearly routine mammograms with no resulting abnormalities, I entertain skipping this year's mammogram. One less appointment sounds good. I *almost* do not schedule.

Expecting normal results, I am surprised to be called in to meet with the radiologist. "I see a couple of areas of concern," he says, his brow furrowed.

"A *couple?*" My mind is whirling.

"I'd like to confer with a colleague regarding the results. Can you come back on Friday? At any time?" Today is Wednesday.

I go home and talk with my husband. We pray and I say to him, "Knowledge is power. Let's put this down until we know something concrete." He reluctantly agrees.

On Friday, I take a galfriend with me. Everything seems to occur in nanoseconds. "I have confirmed you have breast cancer in two areas of the right breast," the radiologist says. "I can recommend a good surgeon and my staff can set up an appointment. The physician I have in mind is well-respected in the oncology community. I'm sorry. I wish I had better news." The situation feels surreal.

At home, I sit with my husband. "It's cancer." We both cry and I say, "Okay, that's it, no more tears. We're going to put this in God's hands and leave it there." I am wrong. I have no idea of the roller-coaster ride we are climbing aboard, following that one little word. We meet with the surgeon who is likable and knowledgeable. Then comes the decision-making. Do I choose a mastectomy? A double mastectomy? Will we forever worry if I chose lumpectomies? What about chemotherapy and radiation? There definitely seems no win-win here. My usual optimism is overshadowed by *what-if's*.

Our adult children have various reactions from, "You'll be alright, it's just a tiny place, right?" To tears and all-out meltdowns. I believe the docs should give you a poster with some diagnoses which reads, "All emotions allowed!" Though we have a team of great physicians, there are no directions on how to do this. I misjudge the emotional travails, as there is no emotion we do not experience. I am moody and agitated, while the depth of my empathy for others is magnified. In this vulnerable place, we are brought to our knees over again. Non-related pains in my body become a concern, if not a paranoia, and each night leaves us with feelings of uncertainty, along with a desire to ensure the well-being of our children and my parents. It is exhausting! After discussions with physicians and family, I make a final decision to undergo lumpectomies.

Following surgery, I leave the hospital well-medicated, thinking, "That part is over." After a lengthy sleep in my familiar bed, I begin to gauge the pain, then slowly move toward reclaiming my body. With my husband at work, I remove the bandages, claiming personal time to process what I anticipate seeing. The result is two-fold. The incisional site is longer than I imagined, though there is only one, as my talented surgeon was able to remove both malignant areas of cancer through a single incision. She has preserved most of the shape of my breast and I feel immediate relief. Prior to surgery, my surgeon spoke with us concerning radiation damage to tissue. "Sometimes radiation causes more significant cosmetic changes than surgery," she said. I'll think about that tomorrow.

We are relieved to learn results from the node biopsies are clear. As radiation therapy begins, it seems strange to be on the inside of rooms I previously viewed only through heavy plated glass windows from the outside corridor. The equipment is huge and noisy. As the technicians position me for treatment, I *imagine* this is simply for research purposes for my book. The technicians scurry out just prior to loud sounds I have only heard in space movies. I meet with the radiation oncologist periodically and, as with any good patient, I have read too much. "I have a question," I tell him. "I know some radiation goes to my lungs. How much of it?" He looks at me a moment.

"As with any treatment, we weigh benefits versus risk. I can tell you the benefits of your treatments far outweigh the risks," he says.

"I understand radiation can itself cause cancer," I reply.

"We carefully determine the amounts you receive," he says. "And, because of research and recent developments, we can direct rays much more concisely."

"But my lungs still receive minute amounts?" I ask.

"Well . . . Just be glad it is on your right side," he *sort* of jokes. My eyes widen and I decide for the moment, I do not need to know it all. Weeks of radiation takes twenty pounds from my medium frame, and my breast is so sensitive, I cannot wear a bra, only a light t-shirt underneath my clothes.

My cancer cells are tested, termed *Oncotype DX*, and results show less than a .5% chance of reoccurrence. My oncologist suggests I begin a five-year regimen of hormonal therapy known as a selective estrogen receptor modulator. The drug attaches to hormone receptors in breast cancer cells and stops the cancer from accessing the hormones they need to grow. After taking the medication for a couple of weeks, I experience blurry vision and discontinue it under the supervision of my oncologist. We restart, with the same side effect, and he switches the medication. Unfortunately, I am unable to tolerate the therapy. The oncologist suggests I consciously tolerate side-effects and continue the medication, though after my own extensive research, I make the decision not to continue. My reasoning would not be another breast cancer patient's reasoning, and I advocate *strongly* that everyone must make his or her own best decision based upon the knowledge at hand. A history of hormone intolerance, as well as vision problems associated with the medication which could be neurological, assisted in my decision. Aware another side effect of these types of medications, though rare, is CVA or stroke, I made a personal decision with consideration for mental stressors continuing the medications could cause.

Medical visits are seemingly endless, and I find multiple visits to the oncologist's office an emotional challenge. The huge waiting area hosts an endless procession of patients, young and old, many having lost weight and hair. Once checked in, we are called back twice, first for blood work, then the doc. The lab is a busy room with nine chairs (I counted) and as many lab techs. I am thankful I have "good" veins, as some patients are less fortunate. I hear one tech referring to another patient, "I couldn't get her vein." I wait for my doc with other anxious people and try to tune out surrounding conversations as I read. I feel embarrassed to be angry, but I really hate this part, a sobering reminder of the loss of control over my circumstances and body. However, it is part of a tomorrow I will have, while others I could even be seated next to may not. I think of the patients to whom I will minister tomorrow. This chaplain is receiving a new education.

Countless individuals own a personal story of each battle waged against cancer. Stories of victory and loss produce heroines, pretty in symbolic pink, as well as men fighting as warriors in battle. Unfolding wings of hope, expressing love and fear—each one heals or makes the journey beyond earth's boundaries. We press on and consider Heaven's perfect peace, for cancer, as formidable as it is, cannot make us go where we were not already bound . . .

As Paul describes the knowledge we will gain in Heaven, certain experiences on earth also cause us to see more clearly. Receiving a diagnosis of cancer is one of them. I have seen cancer face-to-face and look to see what God will bring of it.

There is a tale of the *sorrow tree,* as every person walks around the perimeter of the tree's trunk, hanging each of their sorrows on a branch.

They are then allowed to choose another sorrow in place of their own. Ultimately, each person chooses to take back his or her own sorrow.

I will keep my own sorrows.

41

The Apple Cart

Even a non-life-threatening illness upsets the routine for most of us. Regardless of who is ill or how long the illness lasts, the bills must still be paid, the meals have to be prepared, the kids still need to get to school, and the laundry has to be done. Routine stressors become higher for family members who are *not* in the hospital bed, as daily demands remain, in addition to responsibilities associated with illness. These factors can illicit strong emotions for the patient and family. Awareness, support, and empathy from extended family and friends is instrumental in strengthening those experiencing the challenges of illness. Assisting in small ways can mean a great deal. A simple trip to the pharmacy or grocery store can help alleviate stress. For primary caregivers, a listening ear is invaluable. These things, though seemingly small, are seldom forgotten.

Whether a loved one is hospitalized, finds SNF a home, or remains in the residence, increased mental, emotional, physical, and financial demands upon families as they support and often suffer along with the individual in their charge can be insurmountable. Small kindnesses not only matter, but they also make it possible for caregivers to maintain some semblance of normalcy.

A New Cart

Our journey elicits prayer for what we *know* to ask, though often God's mercies are unanticipated. I share thoughts of retirement from chaplaincy with my director who asks about my subsequent plans. I find it difficult to imagine leaving the medical staff and patients I love, though chaplaincy can also be a difficult role to merge from into something else. Having driven forty-five miles each way for many years, my hope is to find a second career closer to home. My heart would not mind a less intense position. My director tells me he has a friend at a hospital near my home who informed him a patient advocate position is available there. Things transition quickly as I apply, interview, and am offered the job. At summer's end, I begin a new vocation.

God has given me a reprieve, as shortly I will dedicate my heart and mind to other matters. I cannot understand as of yet, a ministerial calling does not end, though it morphs to suit God's intentions.

42

The Abyss

We travel the scenic ten hours to visit my parents at Thanksgiving, celebrating Christmas early as we have come to do. This affords us the ability to stay home and celebrate Christmas with our adult children and grandchildren. Our evening arrival includes only dinner and sleep. The next morning, we begin catching up over coffee, planning a day of my mother's favorite past-times since retirement—eating out and shopping. Normally spry, we soon notice Mom appears *off*. When I ask, she says she has not felt well for a couple of weeks but has seen her physician who told her to rest. I comment individuals sometimes experience *walking pneumonia* without being aware. Mom insists her lungs are clear and she just needs to take it easy. When I inquire whether she received her flu shot, I am alarmed to hear her say, "I forgot this year." Knowing my parents rely upon her expertise as a retired nurse, I learn neither of them have been inoculated. She promises they will see their PCP after our visit.

We return home, my parents visit their PCP, and Mother is hospitalized with pneumonia. In addition, a blood clot is found in her leg which may have resulted from a fall on her carpeted stairs months earlier. Though she did not consider the fall serious at the time, the clot has traveled to Mom's lungs, complicated by COPD from prior years of smoking. She is soon transferred to the intensive care unit at a hospital in a neighboring city, and after conversing with one of her physicians, I travel back to my parents' home with two of our adult daughters to find my mom is doing poorly. Her condition becomes critical, and we are prepared for the worst by the medical staff, though one of her nurses comments, "Don't give up; she's pretty feisty." We *do not* give up, and though she develops atrial fibrillation, the cardiologist suggests her heart remains strong and she can recover.

After six long weeks, Mom is transferred back to a regular unit and eventually to a skilled nursing facility near my parents' home for rehabilitation. Things do not go smoothly as she is readmitted to the hospital twice more before she is strong enough to consistently remain in rehab. Mother has lost the ability to control her bowels, is incontinent, and due to lengthy hospitalizations without mobility, her leg muscles have lost mass and she is unable to walk.

My husband and I keep diligent watch over my parents during the weeks and months of my mother's hospitalization and rehabilitation, visiting as often as possible, as do our adult children. We discuss possible scenarios with Dad from the chance Mom will not recover sufficiently to return home, to setting up arrangements for their needs should she improve. The church offers to help with laundry, cooking, and cleaning.

One Sunday afternoon while my husband and I are running errands, my dad calls. Hearing the stress in his voice, I ask, "Are you alright, Dad?" He is quiet. "Dad, are you alright?" I repeat.

"I don't know, Jan," my dad replies. "I don't know what to do with your mother. She isn't happy and she isn't cooperating. She wants me to bring her home."

"Do you want me to come home?" I ask.

Again, a pause. "Yes," he says.

"Ok, Dad, let me make arrangements at work. I can leave Thursday and take Friday off. That way I can stay over the weekend. Or if you need me sooner, I can leave in the morning."

Another hesitation, then, "Come tomorrow," he says.

I call one of our daughters to go with me, and we plan to leave early the next morning. Once we get there, I accompany my dad to meet with the skilled nursing facility on my parent's behalf regarding insurances and billing. My daughter spends hours cleaning their normally spotless home which has basically become the domicile of a temporarily single older gentleman.

I recall snatches of my father during this time. Taking him to his PCP for a sinus infection, I see him, tall and sinewy, seated in the exam chair updating his mental health form. "Do you ever get depressed?" The nurse asks.

My father hesitates, perhaps for a second too long, then answers, "No, no."

I see him in his home walking down the hallway with his big cat, Moberg, draped across his large hands. "He does tricks like a dog," Dad tells us. "Watch." My father throws a cat toy across his bedroom, where my daughter and I have come to say goodnight. "Get it, Mo!" He commands. Moberg just looks at us.

"You can count on a pet or baby to make you look dumb when you want to show them off," I tell Dad. Moberg jumps down from the bed. At twenty-five pounds, the bed reacts like an ocean wave. My daughter pulls the cover up over Dad's feet. "Don't look at my big ugly feet!" He says to her. My feet are big and ugly like my father's, but I love that they are like his.

Though making some medical improvements, Mom remains uncooperative with staff and refuses to work with physical therapy. Dad shares his frustration regarding her resistance to those things which could improve her health. Mother blatantly tells him *and* the medical staff that she will not cooperate. I ponder this deeply. *Why* would Mom not want to improve? Could this be due to changes in her mental status, or is she simply used to receiving care without being expected to participate in her own healing? A phenomenon occurs at times when a patient is so accustomed to attention and sympathy that he or she becomes, for lack of a better word, "bratty." Whatever is happening to my mother is quite stressful for my father.

More than once, Mom tells Dad to leave. "Get out," is her choice of phrase. The man who has devoted months of energy and worry, and many years of love, now feels rejected by the bride he married at twenty. The responsibilities they shared together, he now carries alone, except for what we are able to accomplish with and for him, largely while long-distance. He expresses his emotional pain in the ways of a strong man of pride, ambiguously.

Two new issues arise. Because of Mom's refusal to participate in rehabilitation and physical therapy, the muscles in her legs have begun to atrophy. Her medical staff advises us it takes approximately five days of physical activity to counteract one day of inactivity. In addition, because Mom refuses to work with physical therapy, there are insurance issues. If she does not cooperate, there will soon be no PT coverage. I tell them we should address these issues with Mother as soon as possible. I realize she is not her normal self, though I am hoping when she hears the gravity of the situation, she will understand how important her cooperation is. The physical therapy director, as well as the director of nursing, join Dad and me in Mom's room. As we sit in a semi-circle around her bed, I gently but firmly converse with her regarding our concerns. To my surprise, Mother is in full agreement. She says, "I will do whatever you want me to."

"Mom, this is more than about what I want," I tell her. "It is about regaining your health. You want to go home with Dad, don't you?" She acknowledges she does. "You want to be in the best health when you do, Mom. Dad does not need to carry you around the house when you can learn to walk again. Do you understand the staff is confident you will be able to walk and return to your life if you cooperate?"

"I want to go home," Mom says, without referring to anything I have said.

"Dad wants you home, Mom. Will you promise us you will cooperate with your physical therapists? Will you promise not to get angry with Dad when he tells you what you need to do?"

"I promise," she says.

We are all focused on Mom.

Satisfied we have done all we can to support my parents, my daughter and I discuss driving back home the following morning. She has a husband and two children awaiting her return, and I am also thinking about my relatively new hospital position. "Do you think we should stay another day?" I ask my daughter.

"It's up to you, Mom," she says. "I don't want you to have any regrets." The phrasing of her words would later become prophetic. Mother has been in a hospital or rehabilitation facility for approximately three months, and we have made this trip often. Because of responsibilities on the other side of our world, I make the decision we should leave the following morning.

My daughter and I are awakened early the next morning to the sound of Dad playing guitar. Since his studio is directly underneath the guestroom, his voice drifts up through the vents. He is singing Waylon Jennings.

Storms never last, do they baby
Bad times all pass with the winds
Your hand in mine stills the thunder
And you make the sun want to shine.
Oh, I followed you down so many roads, baby
I picked wildflowers and sung you soft sad songs
And every road we took, God knows,
Our search was for the truth
And the storm brewin' now won't be the last . . .

We meet Dad in the kitchen for coffee and a prayer, which has for years been our habit prior to leaving. He is in a somber frame of mind, but considering the situation, it is understandable. Before we leave, he looks at my daughter and says, "Be mindful, gal, Satan is always trying to get on our backs." My daughter looks at her grandfather thoughtfully and laughs a little.

"Okay, Big Daddy," she says.

Rather than smiling in return, my dad replies, "I'm serious, honey. Don't forget that."

She looks into her grandfather's green eyes and replies, "I won't." He hugs her tightly, and we get our luggage to the car. The double glass doors from the kitchen face the blacktop drive where our car is parked, and my parents typically wave goodbye from there. After we allow the car to warm up a bit and buckle up, we look toward those familiar doors. My father is not there.

We have traveled approximately four hours when dad calls. I am initially happy to hear from him until I hear the weariness in his voice. "Jan, you're not going to believe this," he says.

"What Dad?" I am somewhat shaken as thoughts of Mom's declining health go through my head.

"Your mother says she is not interested in physical therapy. She's done a total reversal from when we talked with her. She insists she wants to go home. She's not in the condition to go home." He hesitates, then his voice cracks. "She told me to get out again. What should I do?"

I tell him, "Leave. Go home, Dad, order a pizza . . . Tomorrow is a new day."

"Do you really think I should leave?" He is so pitiful.

"Yes, Dad, I really do." I feel anger toward Mom, toward the situation, and toward the despair in this strong man's voice. "Just give her some space. Do you want me to come back?"

After a pause, Dad says, "No, I'll be alright. You've got that new job to get back to."

"Work is work and family is family, Dad. I'll turn this car around if you tell me to."

"No, you go home. I'll decide what to do about your mother. She just wants to come home."

"I know, Dad, but she can't. Give her some time to herself if that's what she wants. Maybe she'll sleep on it tonight and wake up ready to try again."

"Okay," he says, "If that's what you think." After we hang up, my daughter and I discuss the situation as we have so many times. Mom's behavior and resistance to therapy is troubling, especially from a previously reasonable woman and retired nurse. My daughter and I agree Mom needs to gain more strength so she can get back home with Dad.

In less than two weeks, I learn from the skilled nursing facility, Dad has relented and plans to take Mom home with home health. I express deep concern, and though the facility does not believe it is a good idea, they tell me Mother is insistent, and they are trying to work with my parents because they understand my dad wants her to be happy. I believe Dad is simply exhausted. Knowing Mom can be stubborn, I worry rationale is being ignored in lieu of her determination to go home.

The SNF asks me to act as a liaison with home health to help my father understand what is involved. My husband and I call Dad on Saturday, planning on a detailed discussion, though he does not have his hearing aids in and hangs up believing I am a solicitor. When we call back, I all but shout, "Dad! Don't hang up, it's Jan!" We engage in a short frustrating call during which Dad cannot hear, and we are unable to discuss anything in depth.

On Monday, I am working. My husband calls to check on Dad prior to leaving for work, ascertaining his stress right away. Dad is at a loss regarding the situation and expresses worry about my mother's health, physically and mentally. My husband encourages him, "You don't know what God can do," he offers. "She may come out of this." My father values the opinions of my husband, though we are unable to ascertain how much Dad was able to hear. And later, we painfully realize Dad choose not to reveal the magnitude of his fears.

On Tuesday, I receive a call at work from home health, asking if I can set up an appointment for the nurse to visit when Mom returns home as they have been unable to contact Dad. Because of his hearing loss, and considering he is preparing to bring Mom home, I am not alarmed and schedule an appointment for Wednesday. I try to call Dad as I am leaving work, though he does not answer. I am cognizant that he naps and goes to bed especially early since Mom has been gone, so I do not want to keep calling and disturb his rest.

Wednesday, I receive a call from the SNF, saying Dad did not come by the facility yesterday, the first time he has failed to visit my mother. I share my thoughts that he is likely getting the house ready for Mom's return. The male nurse tells me Dad was supposed to arrive to take her home by now, and he thinks something could be wrong. I do as well and call my husband. We both attempt to contact Dad with no result. In lieu of the situation and stress Dad has been under, I am concerned he could have suffered a stroke or heart attack. After meeting at home, my husband and I contact Dad and Mom's local police department and explain the situation, adding that Dad is hard of hearing. The officer shares that he knows my parents because of their involvement in the community and assures me he will sound his siren if Dad is unable to hear the doorbell.

We receive a call back which my husband takes. The officer reports Dad did not answer the door, nor did he respond to the siren. They have ascertained he is in a bedroom as they are able to partially see him through the window and ask for permission to break in to enter. Hearing the conversation, I tell my husband to let them know Dad is a hunter and gun collector, being cautious for their safety, and praying Dad is somehow sleeping through all of this.

After nearly two hours without further word, my husband wants to call the officer back. I am hesitant, fearing they could be performing CPR—more fearful of what we will hear. We wait fifteen more minutes and my husband calls. The officer puts someone else on the phone, a detective. When my husband takes his phone to the bedroom, I know this is not good. From my husband's somber tone, I brace myself that my father is possibly dead. Following the call, my husband calls me to the bedroom. I do not want to hear this. He places his hands on each side of my shoulders and looks me in the eyes. "Honey," he says, "Your dad has taken his life." I drop to my knees, and he drops with me.

"No, no, no," I say. "We do not do this! Our family does not do this! My dad never gives up; he always says, 'Never give up!' It isn't true, it *can't* be true. Please, please . . ." My husband bears the burden of calling our children and spouses. I cannot bear to be in proximity to hear. This is the first moment as a mother, I am unable to comfort my children.

We begin the long difficult journey south with two of our children, as the rest of our family will follow. There are few words, infinite thoughts.

Arriving mentally and emotionally drained, we are intensely aware of the impending conversation with my mother. Because of her health, I question whether she can process this. I briefly entertain not telling her, or telling her an altered version of the truth, though I consider the awful possibility of Mom hearing of my father's suicide from another source. I need to bear this responsibility, not only to tell her the truth but to be there to support her.

Upon entering Mom's room, I see all her belongings are packed. It is a fresh stab to my heart, realizing this is because she thought she was going home with Dad. I sit on the side of her bed and take her small hands in mine. "Mom, I have to tell you something," I begin. "I don't know any way to say this, except to just tell you. Dad took his life, Mom. He shot himself." She looks at me in disbelief.

"Why would he do that?" She asks.

"We don't know, Mom. We don't understand; we're still in shock."

"I don't understand why," she says.

For many days, Mother wakes up forgetting Dad is dead. It is like a nightmare version of the movie *Groundhog Day.* We must tell her over again each day what has happened. Her health deteriorates rapidly, and we do not expect her to survive.

43

The Message

We arrive at my parents' home to find it in near perfect order, as though Dad has simply gone to the store. There is a half-eaten snack on the table, a moon pie. The police told us Dad's clothes were neatly folded over a chair, but my husband will not allow my daughter and me to go into his room. He asks us to stay in another part of the house while he and our son carry out the mattress from the bed upon which Dad took his life. I do not look, but my daughter later tells me she was drawn to the window as they loaded the mattress onto Dad's truck. The bottom of the mattress was facing her, and she saw—formed in her grandfather's blood—the perfect outline of a heart. Tasked with helping carry Big Daddy's blood-stained mattress, my son shared that the pain of it would draw him to God in ways he could only later process in increments. He said such raw emotions formed an eternal bond of respect between him and my husband.

Eulogy for My Father

There is no choice other than to conduct my father's eulogy; I would choose no other person to speak of his goodness or defend his integrity. I deliver my father's eulogy as Mom drifts in and out of awareness. Dad's career as a successful arbitrator has brought past colleagues to pay their respects, and I am thankful for the opportunity to honor him alongside our family and countless friends from my parent's hometown. Neither his intelligence, nor his courage, is left to doubt, as I speak of his service on the front lines of Korea and two military grandsons-in-law fold his flag.

I speak of Dad's talent as a musician. Self-taught as a child, he once told me the guitar had been his mental salvation. His music was a constant in our home, Mom and I waking regularly to his voice in the early morning hours. He sang familiar lyrics and composed his own—a lifetime spent entertaining with his beautiful singing voice. Dad performed with a band for various functions, often donating his time and talent. When he retired at fifty-five, he sang solo in a supper club and recorded a CD played on music systems in local businesses and physicians' offices, and as far away as Iraq. Dad sang of love and romance and songs which told stories. He sang Hank Williams, Waylon Jennings, Merle Haggard, Johnny Cash, Patsy Cline, and Elvis. And he sang for the Lord.

"Precious memories, how they linger;
How they ever flood my soul.
In the stillness of the midnight
Precious sacred scenes unfold."

"His foundation is in the holy mountains. The Lord shall count, when he writeth up the people, that this man was born there. The singers as the players on instruments shall be there: my sources of life and joy are in thee" (Psalm 87:1, 6-7 AB).

In days and months following my father's funeral, my family turns over every rock imaginable to make sense of his death. This is the mental work left behind for families and loved ones following what seems a senseless death. We surmise and analyze, conversing as much as our hearts will allow. Dad had alcohol in his system, likely clouding his judgement. It is heartbreaking to believe he drank to cope and became unable to reason. Whatever burdens were upon him, he drank to attempt to alleviate them on the evening of his death. We believe Dad's perfectionistic nature perhaps played a role in his refusal to accept anything less than the embodiment of what he expected from himself, and thought others expected. He was tired. Maybe Dad just wanted to go home. Our family has worked to understand as best we can, but ultimately, my father took all his reasons to Heaven with him.

Our tragedy was never meant to be. Some things are *not meant to be,* and some that *were* will never happen now. Dad will not give loving pet names to his newest grandchildren. He will not hold them and see how magnificent they are. They will not remember Big Daddy, his delightful wit, unabashed faith, and long lanky arms enfolding them.

We are left to guess, to grieve this act, senseless on the surface, with infinite repercussions. To feel guilty, since the act of suicide delivers guilt to those left behind. Even those with lesser associations ask, "What could I have done?" Ultimately, it was my father's decision, and if it now yields him peace in a perfect place, he deserves it. We refuse to pass judgement upon someone in that much pain, though his actions passed inconceivable pain along to those who love him most. One call, "I am in trouble," would have sent us to him without judgment. If he had divulged his pain, would another stressor on another day have positioned him there again? If so, we would have again been there, ready to help this strong patriarch in his time of need. Search as we may from the deepest recesses of our hearts, many of our questions will remain unanswered on this side of Heaven.

At eighty-five, Dad likely felt a tremendous weight of responsibility. Though we cannot know what another person is thinking, we can be aware that their mental or emotional places may be deeper than we think. Rather than saying he was afraid or uncertain he could face those things which loomed ominously over him, Dad took his life. Those who contemplate suicide will at times speak of it. Years ago, my father said he would allow no one to take care of his personal needs as he aged—that he would take his life before letting that happen. We discussed this statement with my father from all aspects at the time—spiritually, mentally, and emotionally. We even spoke of the selfish aspect of suicide in passing the pain to others. Though, caught in the perfect storm, he could not hear above his own. "Satan is like a roaring lion, roaming to and fro, seeking whom he may destroy" (1 Peter 5:8).

I am certain Dad's favorite verse: "Be still and know that I am God" (Psalm 46:10 NIV) stilled him many times. Though on the night of his death, I deeply grieve he did not listen to the verse he loved—the scripture God spoke to him so often that he hung it on the wall of his studio. How many times could these simple and powerful words save us? *Be still.*

My father once wrote:

> *Jan,*
> *I'll start off by early morning stillness, remembering those quiet moments listening to the crickets and sounds of night with everything settling in—the rustle of the birds going to roost. Of course, I could still hear a pin drop then on Wolf Creek.*
> *We leave those boyhood days behind and start a family of our own, still enjoying those quiet moments, maybe less frequently because of the new responsibilities a family brings. Some of those times were watching you grow up, engrossed with your pretending, completely unaware of me. Watching you—what golden moments. Isn't it amazing? Now I know those moments included God and peace. We go chasing bright lights, money, fame, trying to recapture those peaceful times. Those times, in my mind, were advance payments for future trying times we face as adults. Now I know why I love Psalm 46:10 so much. "Be still and know that I am God!"*
> *All that matters in life is that we realize the finality of a physical existence, and when the spiritual life begins, we ask, "Was that only a dream, and eternity is reality?" I am in Christ.*
> *Dad*

Grief is like a storm. The clouds gather, the lightning strikes, and the storm takes full focus. The thunder, deafening, is all one may hear. Numbness descends like a shroud as some griefs are almost unspeakable. Eventually, cutting through the clouds shines a ray of light, a ray of hope. The air begins to clear as the clouds roll back, and slowly one can think and feel and reason once more. The Heavens shine through, and the hand of God is felt as one realizes . . . it was there all along.

"If you would be a real seeker after truth, it is necessary that at least once in your life you doubt, as far as possible, all things" Ren`e Descartes (1596-1650).

44

Rising Back Up

Too weak to travel, Mom remains at the skilled nursing facility near my parents' neighborhood as the rest of us travel back to our hometown to prepare for her eventual move. When she is stronger, we hope to bring her to temporarily reside in a facility close to the hospital where I work. There is much preparation to do. Added to our attempts to process my father's death and funeral, it feels somewhat insurmountable.

I continue learning nuances of my new position at the hospital, and while my director is supportive and empathetic regarding my personal circumstances, she expects me to fulfil my duties. Perhaps the greatest pressures are self-expectations. Like my father, I cut myself little slack. I briefly consider resigning from my position to care for Mom, though I not only enjoy my job, I sense it will help keep perspectives in balance.

In contact regularly with Mother's present facility, we travel to visit her as often as we can. Overseeing necessary medical and legal affairs, we are thankful my parents organized well, as documents, wills, deeds, and accounts are set up clearly. I think of countless families from the hospital who have struggled without medical or general powers of attorney and make a mental note to update ours for the children. The stressors of illness or death are challenging enough *with* the necessary documents to make decisions. In preparation for Mom's move, we place my parents' home on the market and arrange an estate sale while my husband continues running his architectural firm and I dedicate time to my new position.

It takes weeks to complete documentation requirements for Mom's transfer, and the SNF's, both in her hometown and ours, have been helpful in the facilitation of details. The condition of my mother remains in question, and after much discussion, my husband and I begin transposing a downstairs game room into a room for Mom should we bring her home. My husband hopes the room will take Mother away from the nightmares she has suffered, and soon most of our time away from work is spent planning and ordering supplies and furniture. As the smallest details are ironed out, it becomes a given that, should she improve enough, we will eventually bring Mom home.

As she slowly gains strength, healthcare providers agree my mother is improved enough to make the trip to the new skilled nursing facility. My husband and I, joined by one daughter, make the ten-hour drive to pick her up in mid-April, almost three months following my father's death. Arriving at the SNF to sign final paperwork, we visit with Mom a bit, spend the night at a nearby hotel, and pick her up early the next morning to head back toward home. We consider driving by my parents' home but conclude it would be too heartbreaking for us all. After several hours on the road, Mother is not doing well, and we are concerned what toll this trip will have on her.

When we stop, we discover Mom is soaked through two layered adult diapers as well as her clothes and car seat. How could we have overlooked something as simple as chuck pads? We brought my car, low enough to get Mom in and out more easily, but there is no large surface to change her. In addition, she is so out of it, Mom cannot assist, so we place more diapers underneath her and continue, stopping only for gas and fast food. We have brought healthy snacks, though Mom eats little except for a couple of fries from Burger King. Initially having felt prepared, I am now doubting our decisions. Mother does not sleep and frequently asks about the distance left to get home. My husband assures us all is well, and after several more hours on the interstate, all the while attempting to be positive and encouraging an unhappy passenger, we take our exit.

The skilled nursing facility, within walking distance to my hospital, is expecting us. When we arrive, Mom implores the staff to put her to bed, and she is soon cleaned up, dressed in her PJ's, and tucked in. My husband, daughter, and I yearn for a bed as well, and as Mom falls asleep, we go home for much-needed rest ourselves. The following morning, I am anxious to see how Mom is doing, and arrive at the SNF early to find mom weak and confused. I visit with her briefly, set up her cell phone so she can speed-dial her family, speak with staff, and return to work.

I visit Mom daily, often twice. I assure her we are nearby, though soon she is calling many times of the day and night. I am new to this and uncertain what to do, as my attempts to explain that we cannot be awakened multiple times nightly and still function seem to have no avail. My daughter and I research traumatic dementia which we believe Mom is experiencing. Discovering it can possibly diminish over time, I rely upon our family's empathetic abilities as we continue a path which can only be *learn as we go.*

We establish a primary care physician for Mom, and she is enthralled with his warmth and caring demeanor. During office visits, we discuss practical goals and possibilities, including moving Mom from the skilled nursing facility to our home, which the physician states could be positive. He tells us Mom can possibly regain use of muscles and motor skills, with proper care and her own desire and discipline to accomplish this, which gives us optimism.

Twice, we receive calls from the SNF that my mom has fallen. The bed is high, the floor is hard, and though there are fall pads on each side, she is skinned up and shaken, as are we. She heals well physically, though she calls in the night screaming my name, scared and alone. I do my best to calm her anxiety, as well as my own. As I research the nine medications

Mom is taking, I am convinced the retired nurse who seldom took anything is experiencing altered mental status caused by a combination of her medications, or side-effects from one or more of them. I discuss this with her PCP, and he agrees to review her medication regimen and options.

Mentally, mom is lost and lonely, viewing me as her lifeline. She wants me to be with her constantly, and though I understand, I feel unable to pull away from my responsibilities, however briefly. Driven by Mom's vulnerability, I find myself at the SNF before work and skipping lunch to be with her. My husband suggests he can spend time with Mom after leaving his office to give me reprieve. Our adult children drive various distances to visit as well, and one son stops by often, bringing her favorite, Hardees. Mom has lost so much with which she was familiar—her husband, community, church, as well as her home and southern surroundings she was born into. As her only child, I am determined to do everything it takes to bring her happiness once more.

My mother has one adopted sibling still residing in her hometown. The story of her sister's adoption is one of deep love and family values. Mom grew up with her best friend who often stayed overnight. This young girl confided the dysfunction in her own home to my grandparents. One dark night, Mom's friend came to their home, crying, following an upsetting evening at her home involving alcohol and abuse. Papa said, as she stood on the porch, her clothing soaked from running through the rain, and he had to decide, as deputy sheriff, whether to arrest her father. Instead, he asked, "Do you want to live with us?" She told Papa she did, and never went back home. I suppose things were simpler back then, as Papa said he paid her folk's a visit, and they agreed she could remain. Her parents sent her a quarter once, but never asked her to come back. She grew to love my grandfather and grandmother as her own parents, and once told me Papa may have saved her life.

Hoping a visit from her sister might be the thing to lift Mom's spirit, we call and make plans for her daughter to bring her. We do not tell Mom, and the surprise is well worth it. They are ecstatic to see one another, and the visit appears to help Mom improve as they visit and share memories.

When her sister departs, Mom is understandably depressed, saying, "We'll probably never see one another again." Sadly, she is right, as her sister dies in less than a year due to heart complications.

Our family believes Mom will be better if we can take her home, and we make tentative plans for fall. I envision relaxed time together as opposed to the multiple, sometimes hurried trips to the skilled nursing facility. As Mom becomes physically stronger, we step up work to finish her room, concerned about her growing unhappiness at the SNF.

While getting a manicure, I mention to the technician we are potentially looking for a caregiver. She tells me her husband attended medical school in their native country, though educational requirements in the US prevent him from pursuing a medical career without essentially starting over. A stay-at-home dad while she works, the children are now old enough that her husband could work, if they tag-team the needs of their kids. We set up an interview which goes well, with our one concern a mildly apparent language barrier. Even so, our prospective caregiver appears kind and intelligent, and we are hopeful to work through this. His enthusiasm is obvious, and we make the decision to hire him. Possessing extensive medical training, Mom's new caregiver is confident he can provide physical therapy as well. We are very hopeful.

Bed, Bath, & Beyond likely mistakes me as a stockholder. I want everything to be right for my mom's transition home, choosing soft pinks and grays to decorate her room. An electric lift chair awaits her, as does a memory foam bed with adjustable head, foot, and massage. We purchase a bedside toilet, blue, pretty (as much as a potty can be), as well as lift belts to transfer Mom's small body more easily. The room is appealing and fully functional. In her bureau, we stock sheets, pads, pajamas, t-shirts, and socks.

Hoping to provide materials which will help rebuild Mom's mental capabilities, we purchase books, crosswords, coloring books, pencils, puzzles, and card games. She loves horses, so we order *Secretariat, Mr. Ed,* and other classic movies we hope Mom will enjoy. The room is comforting, touting a wall of windows with remote blinds my husband has designed with an animal feeding station just outside. Our home in the woods near the water brings deer, birds, squirrels, and other wildlife finding solace here. My prayer is that my mother will as well.

We feel sufficiently prepared to begin caring for Mom, and her new caregiver accompanies us to bring her home—his idea. We are excited and anticipate positive results from the education he brings. Mom's first few days with us are busy as she settles in. Home health arrives and as we become acquainted, I find viewing things from the inside brings new perspective—previously experienced less subjectively—on my position with hospital patients and families.

Because my mother has not recently been immersed in a tub, her skin is shedding cells. Even with regular bed baths, flakes of dead skin cling to her sheets and pajamas. Weighing perhaps one hundred pounds, Mom has not regained strength enough to be weight-bearing. Anticipating difficulties getting her in and out of a regular tub, we purchase a soft blow-up tub, complete with a pretty ocean mat and zip-top to keep her cozy. The caregiver and I prepare the tub as if for a baby, getting the water temperature just right as we undertake Mom's first bath time together.

I have failed to anticipate the difficulty of bathing mom *if she does not want a bath.* Her yelling and flailing catch us off guard, and attempts to reason are futile. Since Mom needs to be bathed, we place her in the soft tub, along with her protests. As I begin to gently bathe her skin with baby soap, she reacts as though she is receiving a beating. I stare at my mother as I would a being from another planet, as her flailing soaks us all. I look to the caregiver who remains calm and helpful as we somehow manage to finish Mom's bath. Over the next few months, bath time remains dramatic at best, which I find somewhat confounding as my mother previously loved baths. I have gone about anticipating her needs as though an exact science, though there appears no solution to this equation.

Day by day, we work to adjust—my mom to her new life, without familiarity, and me to the new demands of our routine. Caregiver or not, I have a second full-time job taking care of her. Mom's room is adjacent to the laundry room. If our caregiver is off, Mom calls out as I do laundry, even if I have just left her room. I try to employ the company of our cat to keep Mom company, though he is uncooperative (unusual for a cat).

The weather is beautiful most days on our eastern coast, and Mom's caregiver attempts to take her out in what I refer to as her *Cadillac wheelchair.* She does not like the "walks" and complains of every bump on the paved drive. My husband carries her small frame to his golf cart to attempt fresh air outings, though she yells throughout the adventure. Mom says she wants to go to Walmart to buy new underwear. Though she has soft cotton bras and cannot wear panties in lieu of diapers, she insists there is a type of *cone-like* bra which will give her a better shape. I consider consulting Madonna but agree to Walmart. Unfortunately, the idea sounds better to her than the actual venture and Mom decides to wait until another time, though that time never comes.

Mom continues to call my husband and me on her flip-phone around the clock. (What, do tell, did the elderly do before Jitterbugs?) Isn't she entitled to keep her technology even when her mind is altered by the effects of illness and trauma? I implore Mom not to call us after 10 PM, but she has little sense of time. My husband installs a large clock in her room, though it does not seem to help. When her caregiver is present, he discourages her from calling, though she is defiant. In his broken English, he tells me, "She get mad." I am becoming well acquainted with dementia's sidekick, *stubbornness.*

One of our daughters, a hairdresser, searches online to find equipment to shampoo and style Mom's hair in bed. The undertaking is hours-long, though my daughter tirelessly pampers Mom, engaging her in conversation, sensical or non. Mom tells her she is her *favorite,* and this is exemplified as my mother instructs me to carry the water. The reservoir is essentially a blow-up sink we place underneath her with a tube which drains into a bucket. I am the *water boy.* Mother loves getting her hair done and holds the mirror from her little canvas basket of treasures up to her still pretty face admiring her hair. I do not pretend to understand their exclusive relationship, as my daughter somehow *gets* my mother, perhaps more than I do. I cannot be jealous, as my daughter solicits a laughter from Mom that I have not heard since before my father's death . . .

We install two cameras in Mom's room to enable us to monitor her around the clock. Routinely, her caregiver leaves shortly before I get home from the hospital. When entering the house, I have become accustomed to hearing Mom shout my name as though she is lost at sea. In a way, we both are.

Organization is paramount to my sanity, and I sit by Mom's bed nightly, preparing her medications for the next twenty-four hours. The routine morphs into weekly preparations to make time for Mom's growing needs. My husband purchases our groceries, though I make several weekly trips to the pharmacy to pick up necessary items like diapers, liners, wipes, lotions, bodywashes, and medications. Mom calls several times during these runs, despite her caregiver's attempts to persuade her otherwise. Tempted to shut off my ringer, I worry there will be an emergency. I cannot remember time demands this intense since having children, though this is not nearly as much fun.

Though we incorporate every convenience for Mom and her caregiver, challenges continue. When transferring her to or from the bed, chair, or potty, she struggles against us, leaning back as she yells, "Don't drop me! Don't hurt me!" We assure her, though I confess that my words do not always reflect my thoughts. One day while I am getting her back to bed from the chair, she jerks back suddenly, falling backwards onto the bed as I fall directly on top of her, bringing us face to face. Eye to eye, I say firmly, "Mom, you need to help me!" She looks at me with those green eyes and smiles mischievously. Something about the situation strikes me as funny, and I break into laughter as does my mother. Reminiscent of Tom Hanks in *The Money Pit*, when the bathtub falls through the floor, I am not sure either of us knows why we are laughing, though in these moments, I see my mom again.

45

Falling Back Down

As Mom's cognizance grows more unpredictable, we do not leave home unless her caregiver is present. Long-time boaters, we hire the caregiver so we can go on the water most Saturdays, at times joined by children and grandchildren. Saturday is also bath day for my mother (yes, planned), so we routinely receive calls while boating from Mom as well as her caregiver. Mom yells in the phone for us to come home, that she is alone, although her caregiver is right there smiling into the camera. I consider inviting Mom tubing with us . . . My husband handles it well, and Mom seems more willing to listen to him, so I defer when I am able. Mom does not like or understand the role reversal which has resulted out of necessity between herself and me.

As cooler weather arrives, I am home on Saturdays, ironically making life more difficult for Mom's caregiver. She calls for me when she does not want to cooperate with him or do physical therapy, and yells for me when she does not want to transfer to her chair. Intervening often, I question myself; "What am I doing?" It seems crazy to employ someone highly skilled to care for my mother, though acquiescing when she becomes uncooperative. My husband patiently explains to Mom my need for time as well, as he becomes more entrenched in her care. Mom responds positively to his kindness, though unfortunately begins calling my husband more often at work, at times during meetings. He tells his constituents to hold up a moment, his mother-in-law is on the phone. "I just got back from a trip to North Carolina," she tells him. "I want you to know I am home, so you won't worry." He thanks my mom for this information and rejoins his meeting. *Love during the tough times defines mercy.*

By the time most evenings roll around, I am hoping for a moment to regroup from work. A writer since youth, I laid this passion aside following my father's death, finding it difficult to concentrate on little else except caring for family. My husband sits with Mom in the evenings, asking questions which seem to spur memories of her childhood, life during the depression, and a world different than ours. Amazingly, Mom shares long-ago details with my husband, and though I sometimes join them, I begin to take advantage of this time to seek solitude. In times to come, I will wish I had sat with them more. Realistically, in lieu of mental preservation, I probably would not have, even if given the time to do over.

My husband and I schedule a much-needed *date*. We hire a sitter, plan dinner and a movie, and leave armed with camera phones. The sitter can stay until 9:30 PM, the exact time the movie lets out. We are not worried as Mom initially goes to sleep around 7:30 PM, and as the movie ends, we begin the fifteen-minute drive home. On the way, I check the house camera to discover my mother is *not* in her bed, and she does not answer her phone. My heart begins to pound as the short miles seem to stretch into eternity.

Entering the driveway, my husband hits the brakes as the house comes into view, and we both jump from the Jeep, racing into the house to Mom's room. As the camera reflected, the bed is empty, and we hear a low moaning coming from the far side of the bed. Moving quickly, we are not prepared for what we find. Blood is everywhere, on Mom's face, pajamas, the carpet, splattered on the chest, the bedspread! "Mom!!! What happened!!?" I all but scream . . .

"I decided to get up." Mom factually states. Her lip is busted, as is the side of her pretty face. I sit down in the floor beside her.

"Oh, Mom," I sob, "You can't do this." Once we clean her up, it is not as bad as it first appeared. Home health deems she is alright, and Mom begins to heal well. Since the bed is low and the floor carpeted, we never anticipated an injurious fall, though now we speak with home health regarding bed rails. They advise rails if she will not climb over, making another fall worse. We order low removeable rails as well as a soft thick bedside mat. Within a week, Mom's dental partial comes out, which holds her upper right teeth. Loosened during the fall, her dentist recommends replacing the aging partial. Remaining conscientious at eighty-six, my mother may be unable to tell us where she is, but she can apply her red lipstick flawlessly, as she gazes in her little mirror at her missing teeth. With the help of her caregiver, we undertake multiple dental appointments, and six months later, the new partial is ready to infix. Seemingly a little crazy, I feel an obligation to keep her feeling pretty.

Mom tells us she will never be happy again. She misses my father and asks to re-read his eulogy. I give it to her, then crying, she asks me *never* to allow her to read it again. The following day, she again asks for the eulogy and pictures of my dad. Deeply subjective due to my own sadness regarding both her and dad, I question whether I can adequately oversee Mom's grief. In the chaplaincy world, grieving the suicide of a spouse is considered *complicated grief* without added factors of confusion, dementia, or health issues. I have consciously implemented avoidance regarding my father's traumatic death to remain strong for Mom, so witnessing my mother's pain is nothing short of torturous at times. My husband and I make a decision to utilize home health counseling services for her. Mom sees them once and tells us she does not want to talk to anyone outside our family about her loss.

While seeming to make physical improvements, mentally Mom seems to be falling into a dark hole, and often I feel I am falling with her. I try to turn to God, but I am crowding God out with my stress. We examine options and schedule a skilled nursing facility reprieve available through

Medicare. As Mom is whisked off by transport to spend a week at a nearby facility, she looks like a lost child. SNF nurses regulate her calls and though the decrease in frequency is a welcome reprieve, Mom does not understand where she is, and sounds distressed and pitiful when allowed to call.

When Mom returns, her caregiver continues his endeavor, believing he can help her walk again. He massages her withered muscles, though her skin is dark purple from insufficient blood flow and inactivity. When she cooperates, he lifts her to a standing position, essentially bearing her weight. She initially appears willing though quickly loses her desire and refuses to even sit in the chair. Her body cannot overcome her mind, which ebbs and flows with sadness, and it seems a lifetime since she expressed the goal to walk again to her PCP. Mom no longer wants to do anything other than watch *Animal Planet* or talk to my husband, and my usual optimism has been overtaken by oppression.

Prescribed anti-depressant and anti-anxiety medications following my father's death, Mom continues to battle depression, so her PCP tries a different anti-depressant. Though we notice an improvement, she does not want to take her other medications, which include cardiac and anti-coagulant medicines for still existing blood clots. We find pills hidden in the sheets, and in her little canvas basket of personal items. It becomes necessary to witness Mom swallow her pills, and soon medication time joins bath time and physical therapy in the ranks of caregiving battles. As luck would have it, the anti-depressant becomes unavailable. Working with her PCP, we try two more anti-depressants before one of them produces positive results. The new medication fails to help as much, but it is all we have.

Mom's grandchildren visit often to help keep her spirit afloat. My husband prays with her regularly and in addition, they have come to share a nightly shot of Frangelico which helps Mom sleep better for part of the night. She has developed *sundowners,* a common plight of the elderly wherein confusion is synonymous with the setting of the sun. Mom lapses into an altered state of mind, telling nonsensical tales, while other times she is in a valley we cannot reach, unable to remember details of her day.

On one occasion, Mom beats on her tray with a hairbrush when I am in the next room folding laundry. "What, Mom?" I call out.

"I just want to be sure you can hear me," she calls back.

"Of course, I can hear you, Mom! I'm right here. I can hear you when I'm *not* right here. We have cameras all over the house!"

Suddenly I hear a voice. It is warm and loving, and it is *not* Mom's. "Be patient with her, Jan." I remain motionless. It is my dad. Tears well up in my eyes.

"Okay, Dad," I whisper. "I'm trying." I stand at the dryer and weep.

Following months of angst regarding medications, Mom pleads, "Jan, I don't want to take them." Her physician informs us her medical condition meets hospice qualifications, and I discuss this with Mom. Though she agrees, I question whether she understands and attempt additional conversations to ensure she takes in what facts she can. She looks like my mother, but my heart aches when the dementia patient answers. Vulnerable as children and again as elderly adults, humans often travel full circle. Mom and I are both exhausted from the trip! I consider my dad being in this position and conclude if it is necessary to own the responsibility of my mother because my father would not, *could not* cope with the heartbreak of this phase of their lives, I willingly take it for him.

As Mom's medical power of attorney, what she cannot understand becomes my responsibility. In making decisions for her, I recall advising many families struggling to make decisions for their elderly or critically ill loved one, "Combine your love with the physicians' expertise." When family members experienced guilt with the weight of these decisions, I offered, "You have been placed in this position. It is a difficult responsibility of love." As I shoulder *my* responsibility of love, it feels strangely like the weight of the world.

I have a husband willing to listen and a large supportive family, though not always the mental energy to converse. I avoid burdening them daily, for as strong as our family has been, I would be remiss to underestimate each member's version of this weight. Attempting to avoid making my life entirely about Mom, a mental claustrophobia ensues as I feel unable to escape the stress. Mom's needs feel all-consuming, and if I pause to look objectively at my responsibilities, I worry I will lose momentum and strength, so I switch to autopilot; *all one knows, absent all one feels.*

Hospice offers a very welcome reprieve. We become acquainted with the team and drawn to the social worker who exudes compassion and realism. Other hospice team members become invaluable. A young, certified nursing assistant comes to bathe and dress Mom each week day morning. The chaplain is personable, though my mother soon opts out of his visits, saying, "He is nice, but he talks too much about 'the end.'" The hospice RN is professional and knowledgeable, albeit somewhat distant. I inwardly question if along her hospice tenure she has switched to autopilot as well . . .

As a hospice patient, Mom is removed from medications other than comfort measures. The result is initially positive as side-effects minimize. Mom becomes *Mom* again for a brief period, though soon she is irritable and confused once more, frustrated with her mental demise. One moment Mom is normal, the next discombobulated. Without our knowledge, she convinces her caregiver that she needs extra stool softener, and developing diarrhea in the night, Mom has a poop fest. Her bedding, pajamas, hair, headboard; nothing within her reach is unsmeared. When her caregiver arrives only minutes after we thwart Mom's fun, there is *no* language barrier in existence which would prevent what he is thinking from being understood.

I appeal to my husband perhaps this is all too much, and we discuss a return to the SNF, though we are concerned with the possibility of falls and inadequate care. My husband compares the present stressors we bear to losses Mom has suffered. He confides that when his parents were elderly, he was entrenched with building his firm and regretted not spending more time with them. "I wish I had rolled Dad's wheelchair down the Home Depot aisle so he could look at tools," he shares. This coming from the man who spent every Saturday tending his parents' lawn. I seek out my director to discuss abbreviated work hours, though she cannot cut them. We will keep Mom. We will keep going.

Experiencing an altercation with Mom's caregiver, we will understand months later that stress and exhaustion on all our parts caused the blurring of perspectives. Our caregiver resigns and I hire three part-time nursing students to replace him. They are great, though working out schedules between their classes and clinicals is a new task. Hindsight is 20/20 and I regret not hiring one of them to allow our previous caregiver a reprieve. Mom misses him—his strength, his loyalty, and his ability to care for her familiar needs. We miss him too. Mistakes are easily made while under undue amounts of stress.

As my mother's health increasingly declines, my emotions stagnate, and my sense of humor diminishes. How ironic, the countless times I have advised family members, "Take care of yourself." Easy to say; difficult to do. My husband says, "Do what you need to do to be okay. Schedule nail appointments, massages, go for margaritas with your friends, whatever it takes to regroup." He misses his wife. I have little desire to do these things, and struggle to find joy. I have never been in a mental or emotionally void place like this, trying to survive, to provide, and wondering who the hell I am.

We learn Mom's sister has fallen ill with heart issues, and Mom takes it hard, saying she will soon see her sister in Heaven. She passes on Valentine's Day, and her daughter shares it is appropriate because of how loving her mother was. I feel slightly jealous, wishing Mom was softer, warmer, like her sister, wondering if this would have lessened my stress.

Over the next few months, Mom's AFIB and COPD worsens, and she develops panic attacks and worsened coughing. She has previously refused oxygen and does not want it now. Though the prescribed comfort care medications help somewhat, she develops increased sleeplessness and other side effects. As the cycle continues, we remain in frequent communication with her physician, and the hospice nurses, including a new young LPN, visit often. Due to Mom's condition, the team meets to discuss next steps and agree the implementation of morphine is appropriate. I sit on our front deck with the hospice RN as she relays the recommendation. "My head hears you, but my heart is not ready," I tell her. "Let me discuss this with my mother." The nurse gives me a surprised look.

She asks, "I'm not sure your mother is in a condition to understand or have that conversation. What do you think?"

"She has periods of clarity, and she is a retired nurse. I believe I can discuss this with her," I reply. As the nurse's expression remains somewhat incredulous, I tell her, "I need to do this."

After the hospice nurse leaves, I sit beside my mother's bed. "I need you to focus, Mom," I tell her. "This is important." She looks at me through weary green eyes.

"Okay," she replies.

I say, "Mom, there is a medication your physician believes will help your breathing, but because of your condition, it could hasten your death. Do you understand what I'm saying?" I cannot bring myself to say the word *morphine*. Later I would question not using exact medical terminology. *Did she fully understand?* I would ask myself.

Mom shifts her gaze. Looking straight ahead, she emphatically states, "I don't care if it hastens my death. I want to be with your daddy and my sister."

"Let's give it some thought," I tell her. "Do you think you should sleep on it tonight? I think we should." She agrees, though shortly after our conversation, Mom has several episodes of shortness of breath accompanied by deep coughing. She does not want to eat and beats on the tray with her hairbrush. She asks if my husband can hear her. "Mom, I'm right here," I tell her.

Not breathing well and frightened, her suffering both medically and mentally is more than anyone should bear. With nighttime impending, I ask, "Do you want to try this medicine?" She nods, and I administer a carefully measured dose of morphine. A horrible emotional battle ensues in my mind and heart. Is this the right thing in a painfully wrong situation? We were never meant to experience this.

Mom asks me to rub her feet, and as I massage her small feet, I ask, "Did Dad ever do this?"

"Oh yes," she says. Later that evening, Mom suddenly says, "I'm sorry for our troubles, Jan."

"Oh, Mom." I cannot say more as I lie down beside her.

I call hospice. There is a scheduled regimen the nurse follows during the day, but at night, I follow the schedule. Mother's frail body reacts quickly to the medications. Two nursing students who have cared for her during the past few months offer to take turns spending the night, and we accept, unable to adequately express how thankful I am for their presence. The new hospice LPN, full of compassion, seems to read my mind, and most surely my heart. These nurses will remain etched in our emotional memory.

Over the next couple days, our family drifts in and out with painful goodbyes. Many prayers are prayed. I talk with Papa, "Come get your little girl," I tell him. It is evident that Mom has begun her journey to the other side of Heaven, and in a few short days, her spirit has gone.

46

Reflections of a Daughter

I examine every decision of the past regarding both of my parents. Should I have insisted upon staying with my father when my mother was hospitalized? I feel pain knowing he could not hear well and may have felt isolated without her. Should we have talked more, rather than focusing on his practical needs, and looked more deeply into his state of heart and mind? Wasn't that my job as a chaplain? More so, as a daughter?

Following Dad's death, did we make the right decision in moving Mom to our hometown, rather than keeping her near her home, sister, lifelong friends, church, and most things familiar? Was that a viable choice for us, considering the stressors of separation? Was Mom's loss of my father so traumatic that the move only accelerated her medical and mental decline? I allow *only* myself to carry any guilt regarding the choices in which there existed no "win-win."

We created a space for my mother and took care of the only parent we had left. My solace is God's mercy, and I pray Mom felt that as well, because I remain uncertain that my love was sufficient. I continue to work through the pain, grieving the loss of my mother and father. I attempt to put a period at the end, though a comma keeps appearing.

Summer of the Dragonflies

My mother's love of dragonflies inspired us at one time to buy her a delicate dragonfly bracelet. As Heaven would have it, the summer following her death, there was an inordinate number of dragonflies. Everywhere I looked, a dragonfly seemed to align itself in my line of vision. Several times, I held out my hand, as one of these beautiful creatures would alight on my fingers. I attempted to minimize the significance; however, one sunlit morning, as I drove through our neighborhood Starbucks where I had often bought coffee to bring home for Mom, a dragonfly hovered beside my open window and remained beside me all the way along the drive thru. Afterwards, whenever a dragonfly hovered nearby, I asked, "Is that you, Mom?"

47

Reflections from the Chaplain

More than a year passes following my mother's death when I meet with my friend and colleague, a hospital chaplain. She helps me empathize with my inner child, the one who felt the weight of her parents' expectations, as well as the adult who accompanied her mother on a mortifying journey at the end of her life. She assists me in realizing my parents had responsibilities I took upon myself. She enables me to see the woman and perfectionistic daughter who never stopped trying to please them. And, accepting my humanness, my friend leads me to a place where I can begin to forgive myself, the chaplain walking on the spiritual side of medicine, for what I think I could have done better.

I will keep my own sorrows.

48

I Will Lay Me Down in Peace and Sleep

I am in church. It is old-fashioned, not unlike the small church we attended when I was a child. I have become separated from my husband and take a seat in the far-right pew. As I glance over the congregation, I see my husband in a far-left pew. As I stand to go join him, someone of whom I was previously unaware stands beside me. I look up, into the face of my father. He is as handsome as ever, impeccably dressed in a suit and tie. He reaches down with familiar long lanky arms to embrace me. I smell his cologne. "I'm here," he says. "You've got this, gal." We remain that way, my arms around his waist, for a few precious moments.

"I don't want to let you go," I tell my dad. "I'll embarrass you in front of all these people." As we do let go, I look over his shoulder to see my mom, seated, waiting for him as she always did when he sang. I turn toward my husband and walk to join him. He is seated beside his mother, who journeyed to Heaven years earlier. "Where is your dad?" I ask.

"Right there," my husband points to the man seated in front of us. I recognize his dad from the back, even though I never met my husband's parents on this side of Heaven. Children are seated on pews near us, though I cannot make out their faces. I will later reflect on the miscarriages my grandmother, mother, myself, and our daughters have experienced; God has allowed me to enter this heavenly realm where many mysteries are too great to be envisioned and understood. Though someday . . .

This was the dream God knew I needed—the dream He saved for me. "And behold, I saw in the visions of my mind as I lay on my bed, an angelic watcher, a holy one, descended from heaven" (Daniel 4:13 AMP).

Advice for Loved Ones

Make your decisions as best you can from the knowledge you have, the medical information you are given, and the love you possess. Be realistic. If you find yourself in the position of caregiver, consider the relationship. Whatever it has been, there will be more. If you enjoy closeness, you will continue to rely on that closeness, even when you do not understand the effects illness and disease have on the mind. If your relationship was less intimate, stressors of illness placed upon it will weigh heavily. Do what you feel is right while leaning on those who love and support you; firstly, God. Rely upon those who are wise. Embrace the best moments and prepare for the worst. Allow Christ's love to make up for what you are not, allowing lessons to teach you, mercy to heal you, and faith to sustain you, no matter how hard the journey.

"The same everlasting Father who cares for you today will take care of you tomorrow, and every day. Either he will shield you from suffering, or He will give you unfailing strength to bear it. Be at peace, then and put all anxious thoughts and imaginations aside" (St. Francis de Sales).

Epilogue

I walk into the patient's room. Her husband is resting in the recliner, his hand covering his eyes, weary from many days of his wife's hospitalization. As he looks up, his eyes reflect concern, and more so, grief. His wife's cancer is relentless.

I introduce myself, a patient advocate, and address their concerns regarding pain management. "I can communicate with your medical staff to help you resolve the issue," I tell them. This is the easy part of my career. I can call a chaplain as I am no longer in the role, no longer in the emotional trenches . . . Am I? I look at this man, heartbroken, destined to lose his wife. I look at the patient—sweet, vulnerable, and depending upon him, her champion, to run this race with her. I *know* where they are.

The man looks at my shirt, black with red birds. "I like your outfit," he says. I smile and tell him my husband thinks it is Christmassy. "No, no," he says. "It's very lovely." A miniscule distraction from the realities of their hospital room.

I leave knowing our medical staff will caringly address concerns to their satisfaction. I understand their pain, the grief in oncology, and head to another unit, the cycle of birth in labor and delivery. I walk on, loving these individuals, grieving with them, and celebrating with them on the profound and never-ending spiritual side of medicine, the journey of a chaplain's walk.

"…In Me you may have peace. In the world you will have tribulation. But take courage; I have overcome the world!" (John 16:33 BSB)

To obtain my father's CD please contact:
chaplainswalk2021@gmail.com

References

Bennett, S. & Felder, K (2003) *Exploring the Land,* Littleton, Co: Caleb Project.

Cavanaugh, Brian, T.O.R., (1990) *The Sower's Seed,* Mahwah, N.J.: Paulist Press.

Dictionary.com (2015). *On-Line Reference*
Retrieved from:
http://dictionary.reference.com/browse/minister?s=t

Eisenberg, E. M., Goodall, H. L., Jr., & Trethewey, A. (2010). *Organizational Communication.* Boston, New York: Bedford/St. Martin's.

Grady, D. (2010). *Facing End-of-Life Talks, Doctors Choose to Wait.*
Retrieved from:
http://www.nytimes.com/2010/01/12/health/12seco.html

Holy Bible, *All Versions*
Retrieved from:
https://www.biblegateway.com/passage/?search

Johnson, R. W., Tilghman, J. S., Davis-Dick, L. R., & Hamilton-Faison, B. (January 01, 2006). A historical overview of spirituality in nursing. *The Abnf Journal: Official Journal of the Association of Black Nursing Faculty in Higher Education, Inc, 17,* 2, 60.

Johnston, T.E. (January 01, 2003) FOCUS ON SPIRITUALITY IN NURSING INTERVENTIONS – Prayer's Clinical Issues and Implications. *Holistic Nursing Practice, 17,* 180

Kapleau, P. (1989). *The Wheel of Life and Death*. New York, N.Y. Doubleday.

Nouwen, H. (1974, 2004). *Out of Solitude: Three Meditations on the Christian Life*. Notra Dame, IN: Ave Maria Press.

Nursing School Hub, September 11, 2014. *The History of Nursing*. Retrieved from: http://www.nursingschoolhub.com/history-nursing/

O'Dell, L. (January 01, 2006). Spirituality in Nursing Care. *International Journal for Human Caring, 10,* 2, 74.

Pew Research Center (2013). *Pew Research Religion & Public Life Report*. Retrieved from: http://religions.pewforum.org/reports

Press Ganey (2002). "Patient Satisfaction with Emotional and Spiritual Care" (2003). Retrieved from: hmablogs.hma.com/. . ./2010/05/Press-Ganey-Patient-satisfaction.pdf

Reinert, K. G., & Koenig, H. G. (December 01, 2013). Re-examining definitions of spirituality in nursing research. *Journal of Advanced Nursing, 69,* 12, 2622.

Ronit Elk, Ph.D.a, Eric J. Hall, MDivb, Cristy DeGregory, Ph.D., RNa, Dennis Graham Ph.D., RN, ANP-BCc, Brian P. Hughes, BCC, MDiv, MSb (September, 2017). The Role of Nurses in Providing Spiritual Care to Patients: An Overview. *Journal of Nursing*, ISSN 1940-6967 Retrieved from: The Role of Nurses in Providing Spiritual Care to Patients: An Overview / Journal of Nursing. Nursing Journals: American Society of Registered Nurses (asrn.org)

Simonds, B. (2014). *Nurses*. Quote used with permission letter to researcher.

Strohl, L. (2001). *Why Doctors Now Believe Faith Heals*, Washingtonian

Yoder, G. (2005). *Companioning the Dying.* Fort Collins, CO: Companion Press.